Air Fryer Cookbook

by Wendy Jo Peterson, MS, RDN
and Elizabeth Shaw, MS, RDN, CLT, CPT

for dummies®
A Wiley Brand

Air Fryer Cookbook For Dummies®

Published by: **John Wiley & Sons, Inc.,** 111 River Street, Hoboken, NJ 07030-5774, www.wiley.com

Copyright © 2020 by John Wiley & Sons, Inc., Hoboken, New Jersey

Published simultaneously in Canada

For general information on our other products and services, please contact our Customer Care Department within the U.S. at 877-762-2974, outside the U.S. at 317-572-3993, or fax 317-572-4002. For technical support, please visit https://hub.wiley.com/community/support/dummies.

Wiley publishes in a variety of print and electronic formats and by print-on-demand. Some material included with standard print versions of this book may not be included in e-books or in print-on-demand. If this book refers to media such as a CD or DVD that is not included in the version you purchased, you may download this material at http://booksupport.wiley.com. For more information about Wiley products, visit www.wiley.com.

Library of Congress Control Number: 2020934287

ISBN 978-1-119-69433-5 (pbk); ISBN 978-1-119-69435-9 (ebk); ISBN 978-1-119-69437-3 (ebk)

Manufactured in the United States of America

SKY10084789_091624

Contents at a Glance

Contents at a Glance

Recipes at a Glance

Snacks

Breads and Muffins

Main Courses

Table of Contents

Introduction

Welcome to the air fryer!

Contrary to what you may think, you can do so much more than cooking frozen tater-tots and french fries with your machine!

The air fryer is quick and efficient. In less than 30 minutes, you can create a delicious breakfast, lunch, or dinner that will satisfy your entire crew.

We fully believe that all foods fit (and you'll see that throughout the book), but we want to encourage you to think outside the box when it comes to trying out recipes in your air fryer. From roasted vegetables to empanadas, to baked eggs and vegan brownies, there's an option for everyone when you enlist the help of your air fryer.

About This Book

Forget what your neighbor may have said about the cons of air-fried food and rest easy knowing that because this book has been written by two health professionals, it gives you the facts. This book offers our philosophies surrounding nutrition and health, on top of instructions on how to use your air fryer.

This book is a reference, which means you don't have to read it from beginning to end, and there won't be a test on Friday. You can dip into this book anytime you want, using the Table of Contents and Index to find the information you need.

Throughout this book, you'll see sidebars (text in gray boxes), as well as paragraphs marked with the Technical Stuff icon. Both of these kinds of material are skippable. Now, rest assured, we wouldn't have written this stuff if we didn't think it was fascinating, but if you're short on time and you just want to figure out how to do something, you can skip these items without missing anything critical.

We minimize the special conventions to keep your life simple, but there are a few you should be aware of:

>> Recipes marked with the tomato icon (🍅) are vegetarian. You'll see this icon in the Recipes in This Book (at the front of the book), as well as in the Recipes in This Chapter (at the beginning of every recipe chapter).

>> All eggs used in the recipe are large. If you use an alternate size, the end result may be slightly off.

Within this book, you may note that some web addresses break across two lines of text. If you're reading this book in print and want to visit one of these web pages, simply key in the web address exactly as it's noted in the text, pretending as though the line break doesn't exist. If you're reading this as an e-book, you've got it easy — just click the web address to be taken directly to the web page.

Foolish Assumptions

In writing this book, we made a few assumptions about you:

>> **You have an air fryer or you're planning to get one soon.** It doesn't matter which model of air fryer you have. The recipes in this book work with every air fryer, regardless of the model.

>> **You may be an air fryer whiz or your air fryer may still be sitting safe and sound in the box it came in.** Whichever end of the spectrum you fall on (or somewhere in between), this book is for you!

>> **You want to make healthy, delicious recipes that everyone will enjoy.**

If this sounds like you, you've come to the right place!

Icons Used in This Book

Throughout this book, you'll see the following icons in the margin. Here's a guide to what the icons mean:

TIP

The Tip icon marks information that can save you time and money as you're planning, shopping for, and preparing air fryer meals.

WARNING

We use the Warning icon when we're filling you in on important safety measures.

REMEMBER

When we tell you something so important that you really should remember it, we use the Remember icon.

TECHNICAL STUFF

When we get a little deep into the weeds on a subject, we use the Technical Stuff icon. If you're short on time, you can safely skip anything marked with this icon without missing the gist of the subject at hand.

Beyond the Book

In addition to the material in the print or e-book you're reading right now, this product also comes with some access-anywhere goodies on the web. Check out the free Cheat Sheet for by going to www.dummies.com and entering **Air Fryer Cookbook For Dummies** in the Search box.

Where to Go from Here

If you're brand-new to the air fryer, spend some time getting to know it in Part 1. We cover the basics in Chapter 1, followed by a deep dive in Chapter 2 that gives you the lowdown on not only which foods work (and which don't) in your air fryer, but also how to stock your pantry for air fryer success!

In Chapters 3 and 4, we share our nutrition knowledge with you to help guide you in using the air fryer to meet your dietary preferences. Whether you're trying out the keto diet or you live predominantly plant-based, we've got a meal plan for you!

If you're already comfortable with the air fryer and you're itching to get going, Part 2 has tons of delicious recipes.

Last but not least, don't forget to peek at Part 3 for tips and tricks to help make your air fryer journey deliciously stress-free!

We hope you turn to this book again and again as your air fryer becomes the fun new appliance your kitchen didn't know it was missing!

1

Getting Started with Air Frying

Chapter **1**

Introducing the Air Fryer

I f you're new to air frying, this chapter is for you! Here, we explore the mechanisms involved in air frying foods and show you how to use your air fryer. After reading this chapter, you'll feel confident and clear on how to air fry your food! We end the chapter with a no-nonsense guide to the pros and cons of air frying, so you know what you're getting into.

Getting Acquainted with Air Frying

When was the last time you enjoyed a decadent meal at a fair? You know the kind of food we're talking about: those greasy, fun foods you only get once every few years, the ones that bring you back to your childhood memories of late summer nights spent underneath the starlit sky with your best friends.

More often than not, the cooking method used to make those foods was deep frying. Although deep frying has its purposes (it's an efficient way to cook a large volume of food quickly), it isn't the best when it comes to health.

For years, engineers spent countless hours trying to come up with a user-friendly machine that would satisfy consumer desire for those rich and crispy fried foods, but they had a tough time replicating an appliance that could check all the boxes.

Everything changed in 2010 when a man with a vision, Fred van der Weij from Philips, finally saw it come to life, and the air fryer, as we've come to know it today, was born! Since then, many companies have brought similar air fryer models to market, designed to cook foods in a similar way.

In this section, we take a closer look into what air frying actually entails.

How air frying works

Have you ever seen one of those money machines, where someone steps inside a cylinder, closes the door, and air starts flowing up from the bottom with money flying through the air?

An air fryer is kind of like one of those money machines. When you put your food into the air fryer and close it, hot air circulates around the food and begins to cook it. The temperature of the air fryer and the type of food you're cooking will help determine the amount of time you need to cook your recipe.

REMEMBER

The big difference between air frying and traditional deep frying is that air fryers require minimal to no oil to cook the food. The hot air circulating around the food helps to impart that crisp texture instead of the oil involved in deep frying.

A few other technologically advanced mechanisms are involved, but this is the gist of how air frying works.

If you're familiar with convection ovens, where hot air is circulated (as opposed to conventional ovens, where the heating element is on the bottom), you'll feel right at home with air frying. An air fryer is essentially a compact convection oven.

TECHNICAL
STUFF

If you want to get a bit more science based, what's actually happening from a chemical perspective when food is cooked in an air fryer is something called the *Maillard reaction*. The Maillard reaction is often referred to as "non-enzymatic browning," or basically a reaction that happens between sugars and amino acids in a recipe that result in the end product taking on a new flavor, texture, and color.

Different models on the market

Just like most big kitchen appliances on the market today, the air fryer has lots of options. There is a make and model out there that will suit your needs and preferences. Here are the big factors that separate them:

» **Price:** Air fryers can range anywhere from $50 to over $300, depending on what you're looking for. Air fryers at the higher end of the price range usually have more bells and whistles, as well as a higher wattage.

TIP

We've tested out $60 models and $200 models and can honestly say we've had similar experiences with both. Bottom line: You can produce a quality, air-fried food with any air fryer.

» **Size:** Are you cooking for yourself? Two? Four? More? The more mouths you have to feed, the bigger the air fryer you'll want to look for.

Most models have about a 3- to 6-quart fill capacity, but some of the larger models on the market can hold up to 16 quarts. When you decide on how much counterspace you have and how many you'll typically be cooking for, you'll know the right model to choose.

TIP

Each of us has three mouths to feed in our homes and the 3-quart models work well for us. Plus, we've used 3-quart models before for entertaining family and friends and even with doubling the recipe, it still was efficient and quick to use.

» **Style of cooking:** Say what? Yes, the type of cooking style will really be a huge deciding factor in choosing which model to buy. There are three main styles of air fryers you'll find on the market:

- *Paddle type:* Typically, a self-turning fryer in which you add the cooking oil to the pan alongside the food.

- *Basket type:* A drop-in basket that traditionally calls for multiple shakes within the cooking cycle. This type of air fryer requires a little more attention during the cooking process, but it's also a lot less expensive than the other varieties.

- *Countertop oven:* This model resembles a toaster oven and has multiple uses. Depending on the make and model, they're fairly inexpensive and they usually allow for a greater volume of food to be cooked at one time than the basket types do.

TIP

We've tried the basket and countertop oven styles and found both fairly comparable. The only word of caution we have for the countertop oven models is this: Sometimes the heat doesn't disperse as evenly, requiring the items in the back of the air fryer to be rotated more frequently to avoid overcooking.

Seeing the benefits of air frying

Air frying is not only a healthier way to cook some more decadent recipes, but it's also efficient. Many popular models of air fryers claim that using an air fryer instead of a deep fryer can lower the fat of the dish by over 75 percent.

This actually makes sense when you think about. Let's say you're going to make homemade fried chicken. If you were to use the deep-frying method of cooking, you'd traditionally need more than 3 cups of oil to cover the chicken to allow the cooking to ensue. On the other hand, if you were to use the air frying method, you'd need less than a tablespoon of oil.

Not convinced yet? No problem! Here are a few other benefits of air frying:

» **Air fryers can promote weight loss (for certain individuals).** For individuals who currently have a highly processed diet filled with deep-fried foods, switching to air frying will certainly help with reducing caloric intake. A reduction in caloric intake will inevitably result in weight loss.

» **Air fryers can increase consumption of healthy foods, like fish, shrimp, and produce.** Eating seafood at least twice a week, as well as increasing your consumption of fruits and vegetables, is highly recommended. If you struggle with getting your family to eat more of these foods on a regular basis, then air frying may be the best way to change their appetites (and minds!).

Not only can you put a light crunchy coating of heart-healthy nuts on some of your fried seafood favorites and cook them in the air fryer, but you can do the same with new herbs, spices, and vegetables! This is a great way to explore new vegetables and flavors in your kitchen, too.

» **Air fryers are safer (for the most part) than deep fryers.** Deep frying can cause splatters of exceptionally hot oil all over your kitchen. Air fryers get super-hot as well, but they don't splatter in the same way a deep fryer does.

REMEMBER

As long as you practice important safety measures when taking foods in and out of your fryer (for example, don't put your hands on the fryer basket), you can feel secure in using your fryer.

» **Air fryers can reduce the risk of potentially harmful agents on certain foods.** A compound called *acrylamide* naturally forms on carbohydrate-rich foods (those traditionally deep-fried foods like french fries, breaded meats, and so on) when cooked at high temperatures. Some studies have found an association between acrylamide and cancer. The jury's still out on whether acrylamide actually *causes* cancer. (You can read more about it at the website of the American Cancer Society: www.cancer.org/cancer/cancer-causes/acrylamide.html.)

What you need to know is that air frying is associated with a *decreased* amount of this compound as compared to deep frying, but some may still be present.

REMEMBER

We firmly believe in balance and moderation. We wouldn't recommend you eat french fries (even air-fried ones) daily.

>> **Air fryers can reduce the risk of preventable diseases affected by diet and nutrition.** This varies depending on many factors like your genetics and current lifestyle habits (such as nutrition and exercise). That said, if your diet is heavy in processed, fried foods, the air fryer may just be the ticket to enjoying the foods you crave in a new, exciting, and healthier way.

Not only can you modify the amount of sodium in your recipes and use more fresh herbs and spices to give flavor to the food instead of salt, but you can also increase the fiber in your diet while including more plants in your meal plan. In Part 2, we show you how the air fryer can roast and bake your favorite veggies, too.

Using Your Air Fryer

Each make and model of air fryer has its own instructions, but air fryers don't require extensive knowledge to operate. We recommend that you start by reading the manual that came with your air fryer and getting to know your particular machine.

With that said, here are a few basic steps that work for all machines:

1. **Clean the air fryer basket and accessories (if they came with your air fryer) with hot soapy water and dry with a dish towel before use.**

2. **Plug in your air fryer and preheat it.**

   This allows the machine time to get to temperature before you actually put the recipe inside.

3. **If applicable, select Air Fry as the function.**

   Some models have a variety of selections to choose from such as Dehydrate, Roast, and so on.

4. **Place your food on the wire rack or trivet, securely seal or close the drawer, and begin to air fry.**

5. **Check the food as applicable, following the recipe instructions.**

6. **When cooking completes, press Cancel and unplug the air fryer.**

Caring for Your Air Fryer

You don't have to invest in any specific detergent or cleanser to keep your air fryer smelling like new. Use this section as your guide to keep your new kitchen appliance in tip-top shape so you can use it for years to come.

Cleaning your air fryer

Cleaning your air fryer is actually a really simple task. With a little elbow grease, some regular dish detergent, and hot water, your air fryer will come back to life, even with the toughest of buildup.

We've experimented with various makes and models and had our fair share of epic disasters in our air fryers (think: cream cheese melted with panko all over the baking tray), but guess what? After letting the basket and/or tray cool, we were easily able to get the buildup off with a regular kitchen sponge and hot soapy water.

Plus, even when switching between seafood and a decadent dessert, the air fryer doesn't require a deep clean.

Wipe down the outside of your fryer after each use. A hot, soapy towel is all that's necessary. This helps get off any grease or food particles that may have latched on during cooking.

TIP

Your air fryer manual may say that the parts to wash are dishwasher safe, but we recommend that you hand wash them instead. Why? Because hand washing will keep your air fryer in better shape than putting it through the wear and tear of the dishwasher. Just spend 5 minutes to give it a thorough hand wash after each use, and you'll have a properly working air fryer for years to come.

Storing your air fryer

You can purchase a snazzy air fryer cover online, but this isn't necessary. We store our air fryers on the countertop because, well, we're writing a cookbook and we use them more frequently! Unfortunately, many models are too bulky for under-the-counter storage. Wherever you choose to store your air fryer, just be sure to put it in an area of your kitchen that isn't near your stovetop or oven so you don't get the residual grease from your day-to-day cooking building up on the outside of it.

WARNING

Avoid storing air fryer tools inside the air fryer. It's too easy to plug in your air fryer, forgetting to check the basket first, only to find that you've air-fried your tools. Instead, find a nice, safe spot to store all the useful kitchen gadgets to accompany your machine.

Taking Safety Precautions When Air Frying

You can take a variety of steps to help keep you and your family safe when using your air fryer. Use this list as a guide to practice safe air frying:

>> **Use your air fryer in an open space.** Even if you have a tight kitchen space, when you're using your air fryer, make sure to place it in an area that doesn't have a cupboard or other cabinet above. This way, the heat produced from the high-temperature cooking won't cause your cabinets to get too hot.

>> **Use oven mitts when removing the basket and/or trays from your air fryer.** You don't need special air fryer oven mitts — just use whatever you have on hand that allows you to safely grasp the air fryer basket, tray, or even kitchen tools that you've used to make your recipe.

>> **Allow food to cool before tasting it.** This may be challenging, especially when the aroma of the dish envelops your kitchen. But, trust us, resist! Trying foods that are too hot may result in a severe burn on the roof of your mouth.

>> **Don't consume breaded and coated foods more than twice a week.** "Limit not eliminate" is our motto when it comes to these kinds of foods.

>> **Avoid spraying cooking spray on the air fryer basket.** Most cooking sprays on the market contain chemicals that can corrode the material used in the air fryer baskets. A simply mist of olive oil is enough to prevent your food from sticking while also still limiting the amount of oil used in comparison to deep frying. Invest in a mister that you can insert your own oil into.

>> **Invest in a BPA-free air fryer.** To ensure that you're cooking in the safest model of air fryer possible, make sure your air fryer is BPA free before taking it for a spin. This is easily identifiable on the product specification sheet or website for the brand.

TECHNICAL STUFF

BPA is one of a few chemicals used in plastics that can be hazardous to your health.

Chapter **2**

Finding Foods for the Fryer

Stocking up on the essential ingredients to create quick meals is one of the best pieces of advice we can give you when it comes to making nutritious and delicious air-fried foods at home.

Plus, a well-stocked kitchen helps you cut back on eating out, even when you think it's faster to go through a drive-thru. Using your air fryer and these kitchen essentials, we promise your meals will come together in less time that it takes for Domino's to deliver.

Stocking Your Kitchen for Air Frying

Here's the deal: We don't have a lot of time and we know you don't either! That's why we want to make air frying easy and simple for you. By stocking your kitchen with staples we use throughout the book, you'll feel less stressed about bringing delicious meals to your table in no time.

Spoiler alert: You won't find frozen french fries and chicken nuggets on the list of freezer staples! We want to empower you to create homemade foods from scratch using your air fryer.

Pantry essentials

In this section, we fill you in on all the foods you'll want to make sure you have in your pantry.

Grains

Here are the typical grains you'll want to keep on hand:

>> Bread crumbs

>> Brown rice

>> Couscous

>> Oats (old-fashioned, steel-cut)

>> Panko (Japanese-style bread crumbs)

>> Polenta

>> Semolina (durum wheat used when making pasta)

>> Quinoa

>> White rice

REMEMBER

If you've read somewhere that grains are bad for you, rest assured: As two registered dietitian nutritionists, we're here to tell you that grains are good for you! Many grains are also naturally gluten-free, so you can enjoy them on a gluten-free diet.

Legumes

No, you shouldn't cook beans from scratch in your air fryer — the consistency won't be right. But we highly recommend keeping a few batched cooked dry beans or cans of beans on hand to make your air fryer recipes come to life.

Here are the legumes and beans you'll want to have on hand:

>> Black beans

>> Garbanzo beans (also referred to as chickpeas)

>> Lentils (red and green)

>> Pinto beans

>> White beans

Be sure to look for non-BPA-lined cans.

TIP

Nuts and seeds

Here's a list of nuts and seeds you'll want to have on hand in your pantry:

>> Almond butter

>> Almonds

>> Cashews

>> Chia seeds

>> Flaxseeds

>> Peanut butter

>> Peanuts

>> Pecans

>> Sesame seeds

>> Walnuts

Shop what's on sale in this category. For example, we don't list pistachios, but if you see they're going for a steal this week at the market, pick them up and swap them into your favorite dishes! Store your nuts in an airtight container in the freezer for optimum freshness.

TIP

Shelf-stable fruits and vegetables

Besides having a well-stocked "cantry," we also recommend that you keep shelf-stable fruits and vegetables on hand. A few of the items on our list may surprise you! Many people don't recognize that apples, avocados, and tomatoes should actually be stored on the counter and not in the fridge!

Here's a good place to start:

>> Apples

>> Avocados

>> Corn (canned)

>> Garlic

>> Green chilies (canned, diced)

>> Onions

» Pasta sauce

» Peaches (canned in 100 percent juice)

» Potatoes (russet, red, and purple)

» Shallots

» Sweet potatoes

» Tomato paste (canned)

» Tomato puree (canned)

» Tomatoes, diced (canned, fire roasted)

» Tomatoes, fresh (cherry, grape, and Roma)

Condiments and dried herbs and spices

If you're reading this book, you're a chef in our eyes, so take note of what the "top chefs" we've interviewed always keep on hand. Buying all these items is an investment upfront, but you'll save big in the long run by being able to re-create your favorite dishes from the comfort of your own home.

Start with the following condiments:

» Apple cider vinegar

» Avocado oil

» Balsamic vinegar

» Beef broth

» Chicken broth

» Coconut milk

» Coconut oil

» Cornstarch

» Ketchup

» Lemon juice

» Mayonnaise

» Mustard

» Olive oil (extra-virgin)

» Red wine vinegar

>> Rice wine vinegar

>> Sesame oil

>> Soy sauce, lite soy sauce, or tamari (gluten-free)

>> Vegetable broth

And try the following dried herbs and spices:

>> Basil

>> Black pepper

>> Chili powder

>> Cinnamon (ground)

>> Cinnamon sticks

>> Coriander

>> Cumin

>> Garam masala

>> Garlic powder

>> Ginger (ground)

>> Italian seasoning

>> Mustard seed (ground)

>> Onion powder

>> Oregano

>> Paprika

>> Parsley

>> Salt

>> Za'atar (Mediterranean spice mixture)

TIP

If it has been a while since you've gone through your spice cabinet, do a deep clean and reinvest in some new spices. Dry, ground spices typically lose their flavor after a year or two, so for optimum quality, consider buying them new. You can buy them in bulk at many health food stores so you're only purchasing a small quantity for the recipes you make time and again rather than a new bottle of one you may only use once a year.

Baking supplies

If you haven't taken a sneak peek at the recipes in this book yet, you'll be glad to know that you can bake in an air fryer, too! Here are the basics you'll want on hand to get started baking:

>> All-purpose flour

>> Applesauce

>> Baking powder

>> Baking soda

>> Brown sugar

>> Cane sugar

>> Chocolate chips

>> Cocoa powder

>> Dried fruit

>> Honey

>> Maple syrup

>> Molasses

>> Powdered sugar

>> Pumpkin puree

>> Vanilla extract

>> Wheat bran

>> Whole-wheat flour

Refrigerator staples

From the dairy case to the produce patch, your refrigerator houses some of the main staples your kitchen needs to run smoothly! We have our own individual preferences when it comes to the brands and dietary types of certain products we buy, but we want you to feel comfortable experimenting with what you typically use in your home. Other than a few recipes in particular, you can confidently swap almond or soy milk for the cow's milk we use in multiple recipes.

Here's a list of dairy products to have on hand:

» Butter

» Cheddar cheese

» Cotija cheese

» Cottage cheese

» Cream cheese

» Eggs

» Milk

» Parmesan cheese

» Ricotta cheese

Add the following produce to your shopping list:

» Bell peppers

» Broccoli

» Butter leaf lettuce

» Green beans

» Kale

» Lemons

» Lettuce greens

» Limes

» Mangos

» Peaches

» Pears

» Pineapple

» Spinach

And don't forget the following fresh herbs:

» Basil

» Chives

>> Cilantro

>> Parsley

>> Rosemary

>> Thyme

Freezer must-haves

A huge time-saving hack is purchasing frozen, washed, prechopped, and ready-to-use vegetables. If you're looking for the air fryer to provide you with a quick and convenient meal, then stocking up on these essentials is critical. Buying meat or poultry in bulk and freezing it is an excellent way to make healthy eating more affordable, too!

We recommend keeping the following protein sources on hand in your freezer:

>> Beef:

- Lean ground

- Short ribs

>> Poultry:

- Boneless, skinless chicken breast

- Chicken sausage

- Chicken thighs

- Chicken wings

- Lean ground chicken or turkey

>> Pork:

- Canadian bacon

- Sausage

>> Seafood:

- Shrimp

- Salmon filets

- Tilapia filets

- Halibut filets

You can freeze the following fruits and vegetables, too:

>> Bell peppers

>> Blackberries

>> Blueberries

>> Broccoli (florets)

>> Cauliflower (florets and riced)

>> Mangos

>> Potatoes

>> Raspberries

>> Spinach

>> Strawberries

Seasoning Foods for the Fryer

A huge part of making air-fried foods not only nutritious but delicious is focusing on seasoning them just right. In this section, we cover everything from understanding the types of oils that pair best with the food and the temperature used to cook that food to making your own flavorful seasoning blends.

If you're not feeling confident in your flavor pairings, you will after reading this section!

Knowing which oil to use

Oils are tricky — it seems like there's always a new nut or seed or, heck, even algae being made into an oil for use in the kitchen.

Here's the deal: You don't have to spend an arm and a leg buying oils. We've done our homework. Here are our secrets for the top oils to use and what foods to use them with:

>> **Avocado oil:** We love everything about avocados, and it's wonderful to see avocado oil at most retailers! This oil has the highest smoke point, rounding out at 480 to 520 degrees. Grab a bottle of unrefined avocado oil and use it in

salads, mayonnaise, and to air fry your favorite vegetables and meats. You'll taste the buttery notes of an avocado with each bite.

>> **Coconut oil:** Unrefined coconut oil hits a smoke point of 350 degrees, but the more refined it is, the hotter you can heat this flavorful oil. Refined coconut oil can heat to 400 degrees and pairs well with Indian and Thai foods. The coconut flavor will shine through.

>> **Extra-virgin olive oil:** Extra-virgin olive oil is our go-to oil for most anything Mediterranean. Contrary to what many people think, extra-virgin olive oil is perfect for an air fryer. The smoke point for extra-virgin olive oil is 350 to 410 degrees.

An interesting fact: The chemical compounds that make extra-virgin olive oil so healthy are also what keep the oil stable at higher temperatures.

>> **Peanut oil:** This classic frying oil is a favorite for Southern foods, like fried chicken, french fries, or stir-fries. Most peanut oils are mild in flavor, which makes this a great neutral oil. Peanut oil ranks high for air frying with a smoke point of 450 degrees.

>> **Sesame oil:** High in flavor and in smoke point, sesame oil ranks high for use in Asian-inspired foods. The smoke point of sesame oil is 450 degrees, but because of its strong flavor, we recommend using just a teaspoon or two as you get started, which for air frying is absolutely perfect!

>> **Vegetable oil:** A blend of canola or soybean oils can often be generically called vegetable oil, and these are good to use when you want to avoid adding strong flavors, perhaps with baked goods. In general, vegetable oil has a smoke point of 400 degrees.

Flavorful oils have a shelf life. When your oils become rancid or bitter in flavor, it's time to toss them. The nice thing about air frying is that a small amount of oil goes a long way. For this reason, we prefer buying small bottles of oil and restocking as needed to ensure freshness with each bite.

Invest in a glass oil mister or sprayer, and skip the aerosol canned varieties. You'll save money, it's healthier, and you can choose which oils you want to mist, instead of being stuck with just one variety. We keep three on hand — one for extra-virgin olive oil, one for avocado oil, and one for canola oil.

Making your own seasoning blend

Seriously, this is the best gift we can give you to keep money in your pocket: do-it-yourself (DIY) seasoning blends! Whether you're in the mood for something spicy, Indian, or Italian, we've got a blend for you.

Plus, by making your own seasoning blends, you can control the amount of salt you put in each recipe. If you're on a low-sodium diet, you can omit the salt and recommend your other diners' season with salt to their preference.

Here are the blends we recommend you start with:

» **Blackened:** 1 tablespoon dried paprika, 1 tablespoon garlic powder, 2 teaspoons onion powder, 1 tablespoon dried thyme, 2 teaspoons dried smoked paprika, 1 teaspoon black pepper, 1 teaspoon cayenne pepper, 1 teaspoon dried oregano, ¼ teaspoon salt

» **Greek:** 1 tablespoon dried oregano, 1 tablespoon garlic powder, 1 teaspoon onion powder, 1 tablespoon dried parsley, 1 teaspoon dried dill, ¼ teaspoon ground cinnamon

» **Indian:** 2 tablespoons ground cumin, 1 tablespoon ground coriander, 1 tablespoon curry powder, 2 teaspoons ground turmeric, ½ teaspoon ground ginger, 2 teaspoons paprika, 1 teaspoon chili powder, 1 teaspoon garam masala

» **Italian:** 1 tablespoon ground oregano, 1 teaspoon garlic powder, 1 tablespoon dried basil, 1 teaspoon ground thyme, 1 teaspoon dried rosemary

» **Mexican:** 1 tablespoon cumin powder, 1 teaspoon coriander, 2 tablespoons chili powder, 1 teaspoon garlic powder, 1 teaspoon dried oregano, ½ teaspoon onion powder

» **Ranch:** ¼ cup dried parsley, 4 teaspoons dried dill, 1 tablespoon dried oregano, 1 tablespoon garlic powder, 1 tablespoon onion powder

» **Za'atar (Mediterranean blend):** 2 tablespoons sesame seeds, 1 tablespoon dried thyme, 2 teaspoons ground cumin, 2 teaspoons ground coriander, 1 tablespoon ground sumac, 1 tablespoon fine sea salt, ¼ teaspoon paprika

TIP

Store these blends in an airtight container (like a small Mason jar) at room temperature for up to 6 months.

IN THIS CHAPTER

» Cooking for a keto diet

» Making low-carb recipes

» Keeping your heart healthy

» Getting fishy with a pescatarian diet

» Making meals on a Mediterranean diet

» Using the air fryer on a vegetarian or vegan diet

Chapter 3

Cooking for Your Diet Type

Considering an air fryer but unsure if it will allow you to follow your particular diet plan? Don't worry, the air fryer can produce high-quality meals for nearly every diet out there. From ketogenic to vegan, you can make nutritious and delicious meals in no time. In this chapter, we show you how you can make the six most common diets we encounter in our practices come to life in your home kitchen!

Keto

A keto diet is essentially high in fat (whole milk, cheese, beef, and so on) and low in carbs. The diet encourages your body to enter a state of *ketosis* (in which your body relies on fat instead of carbohydrates for fuel).

WARNING

Although the keto diet has become very popular in recent years among those interested in weight loss, we think you should use caution — ketosis can be a very serious and dangerous condition if not monitored closely. Plus, we hate to break it to you, but more often than not, those who follow a keto diet for short-term weight loss end up regaining the weight (plus some) in the long run.

With all that said, certain medical conditions (such as epilepsy) do warrant the use of a keto diet under the care of a registered dietitian nutritionist.

If you're interested in trying out a few of the keto diet recipes in the book, check out the following:

>> Asiago Broccoli (Chapter 9)

>> Avocado Fries (Chapter 7)

>> Bacon-Wrapped Asparagus (Chapter 9)

>> Bacon-Wrapped Scallops (Chapter 12)

>> Beef Short Ribs (Chapter 11)

>> Crispy Bacon (Chapter 5)

>> Herbed Cheese Brittle (Chapter 7)

>> Jerk Turkey Meatballs (Chapter 11)

>> Keto Cheesecake Cups (Chapter 14)

TIP

To find out more about the keto diet, check out *Keto Diet For Dummies*, by Rami Abrams and Vicky Abrams (Wiley).

Low-Carb

Whether you were diagnosed with prediabetes or diabetes or you're just interested in experimenting with low-carb cuisine, this section is for you.

Before we get too far into the weeds here, we want you to know that there is technically no strict definition of what a low-carb diet entails, especially considering the fact that the number of total grams of carbs needed varies depending on a person's body size and nutritional needs. That said, most healthcare professionals associate a traditional low-carb diet as anything under 150 grams of carbohydrates per day.

REMEMBER

Carbohydrates are certainly an important part of your diet (they provide energy your body needs), and they come in two different forms:

>> **Simple:** Simple carbohydrates consist of a refined, white flour that is fairly low in nutrient density (meaning it's low in fiber and traditionally low in other important vitamins and minerals unless it has been enriched with them after processing). Simple carbohydrates are found in foods like processed snacks and baked goods, white pastas and breads, and other sweet treats.

>> **Complex:** Complex carbohydrates are nutrient dense, containing more fiber, protein, and other important vitamins and minerals than their simple counter-part. You'll find complex carbs in foods like whole-grain breads, pastas, quinoa, and other grains.

Fruits and starchy vegetables are also sources of carbohydrates that provide many important nutrients for your body. Even on a low-carbohydrate diet, nutrition professionals still encourage consumption of these foods.

Now, with all that said, the traditional Westernized diet is extremely high in car-bohydrates. There are many opportunities to make healthy dietary changes to lower your carbohydrate intake while still eating plenty of healthy foods.

The following recipes will help guide you in incorporating more produce into your diet to naturally help lower your carbohydrate intake and fill up with wholesome, nourishing foods:

>> Baked Eggs (Chapter 5)

>> Buffalo Cauliflower (Chapter 7)

>> Honey-Roasted Mixed Nuts (Chapter 14)

>> Gluten-Free Nutty Chicken Fingers (Chapter 11)

>> Pizza Portobello Mushrooms (Chapter 13)

>> Southwest Gluten-Free Turkey Meatloaf (Chapter 11)

>> Mustard-Crusted Rib Eye (Chapter 11)

>> Pecan-Crusted Tilapia (Chapter 12)

>> Prosciutto Mozzarella Bites (Chapter 7)

>> Veggie Cheese Bites (Chapter 7)

>> Zucchini Fritters (Chapter 7)

To find out more about the low-carb lifestyle, check out *Low-Carb Dieting For Dummies*, by Katherine B. Chauncey (Wiley).

Heart-Healthy

A heart-healthy diet is traditionally low in sodium and saturated fat and high in fiber, unsaturated fats, and produce. Foods you'll likely see on a heart-healthy meal plan include nuts, seeds, extra-virgin olive oil, beans, legumes, fruits and vegetables, and lean sources of protein like fish, chicken, and turkey.

You won't find foods that are deep-fried, breaded, and high in added sugar on this plan. But, rest assured, we show you how to make similar options at home using your air fryer!

To get you started on a heart-healthy meal plan at home, check out some of our favorite recipes:

>> Carrot Chips (Chapter 10)

>> Charred Cauliflower Tacos (Chapter 13)

>> Chocolate Chip Banana Muffins (Chapter 6)

>> Honey-Roasted Mixed Nuts (Chapter 14)

>> Goat Cheese, Beet, and Kale Frittata (Chapter 5)

>> Italian Roasted Chicken Thighs (Chapter 11)

>> Roasted Brussels Sprouts (Chapter 9)

>> Wild Blueberry Lemon Chia Bread (Chapter 6)

>> Zucchini Walnut Bread (Chapter 6)

To find out more about the low-carb lifestyle, check out *The Heart Healthy Cookbook For Dummies*, by James M. Rippe, with Amy G. Myrdal, Angela Harley Kirkpatrick, and Mary Abbott Waite (Wiley).

Pescatarian

The pescatarian diet is predominantly plant based, with the exception of incorporating seafood, like fish and crustaceans.

Given that seafood has proven to be such a rich source of important nutrients that are amazing for your health, it's no wonder many individuals who've embraced a vegetarian diet for years are beginning to include more seafood in their diets.

You'll find some of the more traditional seafood fried foods in Chapter 12, with our go-to favorites from that chapter listed here, but the possibilities are limitless when it comes to preparing more seafood in your air fryer:

» Bacon-Wrapped Scallops

» Beer-Breaded Halibut Fish Tacos

» Blackened Catfish

» Calamari Fritti

» Coconut Shrimp

» Crab Cakes

» Honey Pecan Shrimp

» Lightened-Up Breaded Fish Filets

» Maple-Crusted Salmon

» Pecan-Crusted Tilapia

» Tuna Patties with Dill Sauce

Mediterranean

The Mediterranean diet has important health benefits for nearly every person walking this planet and is fairly easy to implement as well.

From incorporating more produce, to increasing your consumption of whole grains and heart-healthy fats like olive oil, nuts, and seeds, to eating fish twice a week and eating other animal proteins like chicken and beef less frequently, there really are opportunities for everyone to enjoy this way of eating.

To set you up for success as you embark or perhaps continue on your Mediterranean diet journey, check out some of our favorite recipes:

» Arancini with Marinara (Chapter 13)

» Calamari Fritti (Chapter 12)

- Calzones (Chapter 8)

- Honey-Roasted Mixed Nuts (Chapter 14)

- Falafel (Chapter 13)

- Italian Meatballs (Chapter 11)

- Mediterranean Egg Sandwich (Chapter 5)

- Mediterranean Roasted Vegetable Panini (Chapter 8)

- Mediterranean Stuffed Chicken Breasts (Chapter 11)

- Moroccan Cauliflower (Chapter 9)

- Prosciutto Mozzarella Bites (Chapter 7)

- Rosemary Lamb Chops (Chapter 11)

- Tuna Patties with Dill Sauce (Chapter 12)

- Za'atar Garbanzo Beans (Chapter 7)

- Zucchini Fritters (Chapter 7)

TIP

If you're interested in learning more about the Mediterranean diet, check out *Mediterranean Diet Cookbook For Dummies*, 2nd Edition, by Meri Raffetto and Wendy Jo Peterson (Wiley).

Vegetarian or Vegan

In general, a vegetarian diet does not include meat. There are variations of the vegetarian diet. For example, lacto-ovo vegetarians eat dairy products and eggs, pescatarians (covered earlier) eat fish, and so on.

A vegan diet, on the other hand, does not include any animal products whatsoever, including dairy, eggs, honey, and so on.

The following recipes will help you begin to explore a plant-forward eating style and even show you the nutritious and delicious recipes that fall under a vegan diet:

- Almond Cranberry Granola (Chapter 5)

- Avocado Egg Rolls (Chapter 7)

- Baked Eggs (Chapter 5)

- Basic Fried Tofu (Chapter 13)

- Spicy Sesame Tempeh Slaw with Peanut Dressing (Chapter 13)
- Beet Chips (Chapter 10)
- Black Bean Empanadas (Chapter 13)
- Cajun Breakfast Potatoes (Chapter 5)
- Cinnamon Apple Crisps (Chapter 10)
- Classic Potato Chips (Chapter 10)
- Corn Tortilla Chips (Chapter 10)
- Falafel (Chapter 13)
- Garlic Parmesan Kale Chips (Chapter 10)
- Lentil Fritters (Chapter 13)
- Street Corn (Chapter 9)
- Tandoori Paneer Naan Pizza (Chapter 13)
- Tempura Fried Veggies (Chapter 7)
- Thai Peanut Veggie Burgers (Chapter 13)
- Apple and Cheddar Grilled Cheese (Chapter 8)
- Vegan Brownie Bites (Chapter 14)

TIP

To find out more about vegetarian cooking, check out *Vegetarian Cooking For Dummies*, by Suzanne Havala (Wiley). And to find out more about vegan cooking, check out *Vegan Cooking For Dummies*, by Alexandra Jamieson (Wiley).

Chapter **4**

Planning Air-Fried Meals

I f you like a set menu guide to follow, this chapter is for you! Here, we pull together sample seven-day meal plans to help guide you in using your air fryer as a part of your weekly meal planning. Whether you're cooking for yourself or an entire family, these plans can be tailored to meet your needs.

REMEMBER

You can adjust a recipe yield by increasing or decreasing the ingredients. Most recipes serve four to six people, so if you're cooking for yourself and you'd prefer to have leftovers for just a couple days, just cut the ingredients in half. Likewise, double the recipe ingredients if you want to double the yield!

TIP

You can create your own meal plan template on a computer, tablet, or phone, or just jot it down on a piece of paper to hang on your fridge!

Note: Throughout this chapter, each recipe title is in bold, followed by the chapter where that recipe appears. Anything not in bold is not a recipe in this book.

A Family-Friendly Meal Plan

Whether you're a family of two or ten, this meal plan is for you.

TIP

Create variety with a build-your-own option. Whether it's a make-your-own-salad, bowl, or yogurt parfait, giving people options empowers them to choose what they like while preventing you from being a short-order cook. Keep meals joyful and not stressful, and you'll be well on your way to having healthy, happy eaters.

REMEMBER

Make food fun! The air fryer can certainly bring fun foods into your meal plan on a weekly basis while also getting your family involved in the cooking process.

Table 4-1 provides a meal plan that'll work for any family.

REMEMBER

Empower your family by letting them build their own meals!

TABLE 4-1   **A Family-Friendly Meal Plan**

	Breakfast	Lunch	Dinner	Snack or Dessert
Monday	Fruit and yogurt parfait with **Almond Cranberry Granola (Chapter 5)**	Lentil soup with toasted bread	**Southwest Gluten-Free Turkey Meat-loaf (Chapter 11)** with side salad	Air-popped popcorn
Tuesday	**Baked Eggs (Chapter 5)** with whole-grain toast and fruit	Leftover meatloaf with side salad	Lentil soup with toasted bread	**Honey-Roasted Mixed Nuts (Chapter 14)**
Wednesday	**Chocolate Chip Banana Muffins (Chapter 6)** with milk	Chicken salad with Greek dressing and a piece of fruit	**Falafel (Chapter 13)** with **Parmesan Garlic Naan (Chapter 6)**	**Cinnamon Apple Crisps (Chapter 10)**
Thursday	Fruit and yogurt parfait with **Almond Cranberry Granola (Chapter 5)**	Leftover falafel with side salad	**Tuna Patties with Dill Sauce (Chapter 12)** with coleslaw	**Chocolate Chip Banana Muffins (Chapter 6)** with milk
Friday	**Baked Eggs (Chapter 5)** with whole-grain toast and fruit	Leftover tuna patty with coleslaw	**Build Your Own Hot Pocket (Chapter 8)** with side salad	**Honey-Roasted Mixed Nuts (Chapter 14)**
Saturday	**French Toast Sticks (Chapter 5)** with fresh fruit	**Veggie Cheese Bites (Chapter 7)** with hummus and fresh vegetables	Turkey burgers with **Panko-Crusted Zucchini Fries (Chapter 9)**	**Baked Apple Crisp (Chapter 14)**
Sunday	**Farmers Market Quiche (Chapter 5)**	Deli turkey sand-wiches with **Root Vegetable Crisps (Chapter 10)**	**Beer-Breaded Halibut Fish Tacos (Chapter 12)** with guacamole and salsa	**Chocolate Chip Banana Muffins (Chapter 6)** with milk

A Mediterranean Diet Meal Plan

The Mediterranean Diet is pretty much the gold standard when it comes to diets for leading your healthiest life yet. All foods are permitted, within reason, with an emphasis on produce, whole grains, nuts and seeds, and heart-healthy fats.

With that said, the air fryer can certainly help you plan out a Mediterranean Diet menu with ease. Take a look at our sample menu in Table 4-2 and see how delicious and nutritious eating like a Mediterranean can be!

TABLE 4-2   **A Mediterranean Diet Meal Plan**

	Breakfast	Lunch	Dinner	Snack or Dessert
Monday	**Mediterranean Egg Sandwich (Chapter 5)**	Lentil soup with toasted bread	**Mediterranean Stuffed Chicken Breasts (Chapter 11)**	Walnut-stuffed dates
Tuesday	Fruit and yogurt parfait with **Almond Cranberry Granola (Chapter 5)**	**Falafel (Chapter 13)** with Greek salad	**Calzones (Chapter 8)** with green salad and Italian vinaigrette	Fresh fruit
Wednesday	**Farmers Market Quiche (Chapter 5)**	**Zucchini Fritters (Chapter 7)** with marinara dipping sauce and **Honey-Roasted Mixed Nuts (Chapter 14)**	**Pizza Portobello Mushrooms (Chapter 13)** and garden salad with fresh bread	Berries and biscotti
Thursday	Boiled eggs with prosciutto and biscotti	**Mediterranean Roasted Vegetable Panini (Chapter 8)**	**Rosemary Lamb Chops (Chapter 11)** with **Crispy Herbed Potatoes (Chapter 9)** and **Asiago Broccoli (Chapter 9)**	½ ounce dark chocolate (70% cacao) and almonds
Friday	Fruit and yogurt parfait with **Almond Cranberry Granola (Chapter 5)**	**Prosciutto Mozzarella Bites (Chapter 7)** with sliced avocado and olives	Grilled white fish with **Za'atar Garbanzo Beans (Chapter 7)** and arugula salad with lemon dressing	Fresh fruit
Saturday	**Mediterranean Egg Sandwich (Chapter 5)**	Warm pita bread with hummus and fresh vegetables	**Italian Meatballs (Chapter 11)** with marinara sauce and wilted spinach	Berries and biscotti
Sunday	**Goat Cheese, Beet, and Kale Frittata (Chapter 5)**	**Mediterranean Roasted Vegetable Panini (Chapter 8)**	Grilled beef tenderloin with **Moroccan Cauliflower (Chapter 9)** and sliced cucumbers and tomatoes	½ ounce dark chocolate (70% cacao) and almonds

The Mediterranean diet doesn't mean drink wine and eat dark chocolate all day (though both are permitted on the diet). Planning out your menu ahead of time will allow you to enjoy a wide variety of seasonal produce with your meals (while saving you money by shopping what's in season).

A Modified Keto Meal Plan

We've created the meal plan in Table 4-3 with the understanding that not every recipe as it's written is 100 percent keto compliant. However, with a few modifications (like omitting the sugar and using an approved keto sweetener, like stevia or monk fruit, or swapping out a grain for cauliflower or lettuce), you can tailor the recipes to a keto diet.

Keto means high fat, so you need to increase the fat of many (if not all) of the recipes in this seven-day meal plan by adding an approved keto fat source. These fat sources include oils (like avocado and olive), as well as high-fat foods like nuts, avocados, and seeds.

TABLE 4-3   ## A Modified Keto Meal Plan

	Breakfast	Lunch	Dinner	Snack or Dessert
Monday	**Crispy Bacon (Chapter 5)** with fried eggs	**Herbed Cheese Brittle (Chapter 7)** with grilled chicken salad	**Beef Short Ribs (Chapter 11)** with **Asiago Broccoli (Chapter 9)** and cauliflower rice	**Honey-Roasted Mixed Nuts (Chapter 14)**
Tuesday	Plain whole milk yogurt with sliced avocado, tomatoes, and walnuts	Leftover short ribs over garden salad with avocado slices	**Herbed Cheese Brittle (Chapter 7)** with grilled chicken salad	**Keto Cheesecake Cups (Chapter 14)**
Wednesday	**Crispy Bacon (Chapter 5)** with fried eggs	Deli meat and cheese roll-ups with celery sticks	**Gluten-Free Nutty Chicken Fingers (Chapter 11)** with vegetables	**Honey-Roasted Mixed Nuts (Chapter 14)**
Thursday	Plain whole milk yogurt with sliced avocado, tomatoes, and walnuts	Leftover chicken fingers over garden salad with oil-based dressing	**Rosemary Lamb Chops (Chapter 11)** with cauliflower rice	**Keto Cheesecake Cups (Chapter 14)**

	Breakfast	Lunch	Dinner	Snack or Dessert
Friday	**Goat Cheese, Beet, and Kale Frittata (Chapter 5; omit the beets)** with sliced avocado	Ground meat with leftover cauliflower rice and steamed vegetables	**Blackened Catfish (Chapter 12)** wrapped in butter leaf lettuce with guacamole and sliced tomatoes	**Honey-Roasted Mixed Nuts (Chapter 14)**
Saturday	**Baked Eggs (Chapter 5)** with avocado	Leftover frittata with side salad	Ground meat with leftover cauliflower rice and steamed vegetables	**Keto Cheesecake Cups (Chapter 14)**
Sunday	**Zucchini Walnut Bread (Chapter 6)** made with almond flour and stevia	Deli meat and cheese roll-ups with celery sticks	**Bacon-Wrapped Scallops (Chapter 12)** with steamed vegetables	**Avocado Fries (Chapter 7)**

A Vegetarian Meal Plan

If you're a vegetarian, the meal plan in Table 4-4 is for you!

TIP

If you're a vegan, take a look at the recipes and see how you can modify them to meet your needs. You can modify many recipes that call for dairy by using a plant-based alternative product, such as an almond or soy milk, yogurt, or butter alternative.

TABLE 4-4   **A Vegetarian Meal Plan**

	Breakfast	Lunch	Dinner	Snack or Dessert
Monday	**Carrot Orange Muffins (Chapter 6)**	**Spicy Sesame Tempeh Slaw with Peanut Dressing (Chapter 13)**	Mediterranean salad with feta, garbanzo beans and Greek dressing, serve with **Parmesan Garlic Naan (Chapter 6)**	**Vegan Brownie Bites (Chapter 14)**
Tuesday	Peanut butter toast with fresh sliced banana	**Eggplant Parmesan (Chapter 13)** with side salad	Leftover tempeh bowls	**Carrot Orange Muffins (Chapter 6)**
Wednesday	**Basic Fried Tofu (Chapter 13)** scrambled with roasted vegetables	Peanut butter sandwich with hummus and carrots	**Black Bean Empanadas (Chapter 13)** with Mexican Caesar salad	**Vegan Brownie Bites (Chapter 14)**

(continued)

TABLE 4-4 *(continued)*

	Breakfast	Lunch	Dinner	Snack or Dessert
Thursday	**Farmers Market Quiche (Chapter 5)**	**Lentil Fritters (Chapter 13)** with side salad	Vegetable soup	**Wild Blueberry Sweet Empanadas (Chapter 14)**
Friday	Leftover quiche with fresh fruit	Leftover fritter on hamburger bun with lettuce and tomato	**Roasted Vegetable Pita Pizza (Chapter 13)**	Air-popped popcorn
Saturday	Avocado toast with sliced tomatoes and hemp seeds	Peanut butter sandwich with hummus and carrots	**Charred Cauliflower Tacos (Chapter 13)** with black beans, corn, and rice mixture	**Wild Blueberry Sweet Empanadas (Chapter 14)**
Sunday	**Carrot Orange Muffins (Chapter 6)**	Leftover cauliflower tacos and salad	**Arancini with Marinara (Chapter 13)** and side salad	**Vegan Brownie Bites (Chapter 14)**

2

Putting the Air Fryer to Work

Chapter 5

Breakfast Staples

I f you aren't a breakfast person, that just might change when you have an air fryer! The breakfast recipes in this chapter aren't your traditional breakfast fare (although you'll find some of those, too.) Think outside the bowl with savory eats like Egg and Sausage Crescent Rolls or Breakfast Chimichangas.

Prefer something sweet to go with your morning cup of joe? We've got that, too. From Apple Fritters to Coffee Cake, there are endless possibilities to satisfy your sweet treat with a healthy air-fried twist!

Baked Eggs

PREP TIME: 5 MIN | **COOK TIME: 6 MIN** | **YIELD: 4 SERVINGS**

INGREDIENTS

4 large eggs

⅛ teaspoon black pepper

⅛ teaspoon salt

DIRECTIONS

1 Preheat the air fryer to 330 degrees. Place 4 silicone muffin liners into the air fryer basket.

2 Crack 1 egg at a time into each silicone muffin liner. Sprinkle with black pepper and salt.

3 Bake for 6 minutes. Remove and let cool 2 minutes prior to serving.

NOTE: Adjust the cooking time based on the desired doneness of the egg yolk — 5 minutes for a soft center, 7 minutes for a hard center.

TIP: Serve alongside a cup of fruit and toast, or place in between a toasted English muffin and top with a slice of cheese for a quick breakfast sandwich on the go.

VARY IT! Scramble eggs first and add chopped spinach and shredded cheese to the eggs. Portion evenly into silicone muffin liners and cook.

Crispy Bacon

PREP TIME: 2 MIN	COOK TIME: 20 MIN	YIELD: 6 SERVINGS

INGREDIENTS

12 ounces bacon

DIRECTIONS

1 Preheat the air fryer to 350 degrees for 3 minutes.

2 Lay out the bacon in a single layer, slightly overlapping the strips of bacon.

3 Air fry for 10 minutes or until desired crispness.

4 Repeat until all the bacon has been cooked.

NOTE: Sizes of air fryers vary. If you overcrowd the pan, it may take longer to cook.

NOTE: If smokiness is an issue, try adding 1 tablespoon of water to the drip pan or bottom of the air fryer prior to cooking.

TIP: Air fryers vary, so be sure to watch yours closely as you cook bacon the first time; yours may cook faster than we've estimated.

VARY IT! If you enjoy a sweet bacon, use a pastry brush to add a touch of maple syrup to the bacon after cooking.

Cajun Breakfast Potatoes

PREP TIME: 5 MIN | COOK TIME: 20 MIN | YIELD: 4 SERVINGS

INGREDIENTS

1 pound roasting potatoes (like russet), scrubbed clean

1 tablespoon vegetable oil

2 teaspoons paprika

½ teaspoon garlic powder

¼ teaspoon onion powder

¼ teaspoon ground cumin

1 teaspoon thyme

1 teaspoon sea salt

½ teaspoon black pepper

DIRECTIONS

1 Cut the potatoes into 1-inch cubes.

2 In a large bowl, toss the cut potatoes with vegetable oil.

3 Sprinkle paprika, garlic powder, onion powder, cumin, thyme, salt, and pepper onto the potatoes, and toss to coat well.

4 Preheat the air fryer to 400 degrees for 4 minutes.

5 Add the potatoes to the air fryer basket and bake for 10 minutes. Stir or toss the potatoes and continue baking for an additional 5 minutes. Stir or toss again and continue baking for an additional 5 minutes or until the desired crispness is achieved.

Farmers Market Quiche

PREP TIME: 15 MIN	COOK TIME: 35 MIN	YIELD: 4 SERVINGS

INGREDIENTS

4 button mushrooms

¼ medium red bell pepper

1 teaspoon extra-virgin olive oil

One 9-inch pie crust, at room temperature

¼ cup grated carrot

¼ cup chopped, fresh baby spinach leaves

3 eggs, whisked

¼ cup half-and-half

½ teaspoon thyme

½ teaspoon sea salt

2 ounces crumbled goat cheese or feta

DIRECTIONS

1 In a medium bowl, toss the mushrooms and bell pepper with extra-virgin olive oil; place into the air fryer basket. Set the temperature to 400 degrees for 8 minutes, stirring after 4 minutes. Remove from the air fryer, and roughly chop the mushrooms and bell peppers. Wipe the air fryer clean.

2 Prep a 7-inch oven-safe baking dish by spraying the bottom of the pan with cooking spray.

3 Place the pie crust into the baking dish; fold over and crimp the edges or use a fork to press to give the edges some shape.

4 In a medium bowl, mix together the mushrooms, bell peppers, carrots, spinach, and eggs. Stir in the half-and-half, thyme, and salt.

5 Pour the quiche mixture into the base of the pie shell. Top with crumbled cheese.

6 Place the quiche into the air fryer basket. Set the temperature to 325 degrees for 30 minutes.

7 When complete, turn the quiche halfway and cook an additional 5 minutes. Allow the quiche to rest 20 minutes prior to slicing and serving.

NOTE: If your air fryer runs hot, drop the temperature to 300 degrees and air fry for a total of 40 minutes or until completely cooked.

NOTE: If your air fryer is smaller, opt to make individual quiches in ramekins instead.

TIP: If the edges of the crust looks crispy, cover with foil.

VARY IT! Go Greek by adding in chopped black olives and feta cheese.

VARY IT! Craving something healthier or short on time? Ditch the crust and make a frittata instead. Increase the temperature to 330 degrees and air fry for 8 minutes.

Goat Cheese, Beet, and Kale Frittata

PREP TIME: 5 MIN	COOK TIME: 20 MIN	YIELD: 6 SERVINGS

INGREDIENTS

6 large eggs

½ teaspoon garlic powder

¼ teaspoon black pepper

¼ teaspoon salt

1 cup chopped kale

1 cup cooked and chopped red beets

⅓ cup crumbled goat cheese

DIRECTIONS

1 Preheat the air fryer to 320 degrees.

2 In a medium bowl, whisk the eggs with the garlic powder, pepper, and salt. Mix in the kale, beets, and goat cheese.

3 Spray an oven-safe 7-inch springform pan with cooking spray. Pour the egg mixture into the pan and place it in the air fryer basket.

4 Cook for 20 minutes, or until the internal temperature reaches 145 degrees.

5 When the frittata is cooked, let it set for 5 minutes before removing from the pan.

6 Slice and serve immediately.

NOTE: Look for a precooked red beet in the refrigerated section of your grocery store to save time. If you can't find crumbled goat cheese, simply buy the goat cheese log and crumble your own.

TIP: Serve alongside a side salad or fresh fruit cup.

VARY IT! Prefer cheddar cheese, bell peppers, and spinach? Use what you like or have on hand!

Breakfast Pot Pies

PREP TIME: 5 MIN | COOK TIME: 20 MIN | YIELD: 4 SERVINGS

INGREDIENTS

1 refrigerated pie crust

½ pound pork breakfast sausage

¼ cup diced onion

1 garlic clove, minced

½ teaspoon ground black pepper

¼ teaspoon salt

1 cup chopped bell peppers

1 cup roasted potatoes

2 cups milk

2 to 3 tablespoons all-purpose flour

DIRECTIONS

1 Flatten the store-bought pie crust out on an even surface. Cut 4 equal circles that are slightly larger than the circumference of ramekins (by about ¼ inch). Set aside.

2 In a medium pot, sauté the breakfast sausage with the onion, garlic, black pepper, and salt. When browned, add in the bell peppers and potatoes and cook an additional 3 to 4 minutes to soften the bell peppers. Remove from the heat and portion equally into the ramekins.

3 To the same pot (without washing it), add the milk. Heat over medium-high heat until boiling. Slowly reduce to a simmer and stir in the flour, 1 tablespoon at a time, until the gravy thickens and coats the back of a wooden spoon (about 5 minutes).

4 Remove from the heat and equally portion ½ cup of gravy into each ramekin on top of the sausage and potato mixture.

5 Place the circle pie crusts on top of the ramekins, lightly pressing them down on the perimeter of each ramekin with the prongs of a fork. Gently poke the prongs into the center top of the pie crust a few times to create holes for the steam to escape as the pie cooks.

6 Bake in the air fryer for 6 minutes (or until the tops are golden brown).

7 Remove and let cool 5 minutes before serving.

NOTE: If you don't have any roasted potatoes already cooked and are tight on time, feel free to substitute this with another root vegetable you already have prepared.

TIP: Serve alongside a fresh side salad or cup of seasonal fruit.

TIP: Do not discard the extra pie crust! Roll it out into a flat rectangle and top with cinnamon, sugar and nuts. Roll up and slice into mini pie crust cookies. Bake at 320 degrees for 5 to 7 minutes.

VARY IT! Swap pork for chicken or alternate your vegetables!

Breakfast Chimichangas

PREP TIME: 10 MIN	COOK TIME: 8 MIN	YIELD: 4 SERVINGS

INGREDIENTS

Four 8-inch flour tortillas

½ cup canned refried beans

1 cup scrambled eggs

½ cup grated cheddar or Monterey jack cheese

1 tablespoon vegetable oil

1 cup salsa

DIRECTIONS

1 Lay the flour tortillas out flat on a cutting board. In the center of each tortilla, spread 2 tablespoons refried beans. Next, add ¼ cup eggs and 2 tablespoons cheese to each tortilla.

2 To fold the tortillas, begin on the left side and fold to the center (see Figure 5-1). Then fold the right side into the center. Next fold the bottom and top down and roll over to completely seal the chimichanga. Using a pastry brush or oil mister, brush the tops of the tortilla packages with oil.

3 Preheat the air fryer to 400 degrees for 4 minutes. Place the chimichangas into the air fryer basket, seam side down, and air fry for 4 minutes. Using tongs, turn over the chimichangas and cook for an additional 2 to 3 minutes or until light golden brown.

TIP: Serve with guacamole, salsa, and sour cream for a hearty breakfast.

VARY IT! Swap out beans with breakfast potatoes or rice.

FIGURE 5-1:
How to fold
a burrito.

Egg and Sausage Crescent Rolls

PREP TIME: 10 MIN   COOK TIME: 11 MIN   YIELD: 8 SERVINGS

INGREDIENTS

5 large eggs

¼ teaspoon black pepper

¼ teaspoon salt

1 tablespoon milk

¼ cup shredded cheddar cheese

One 8-ounce package refrigerated crescent rolls

4 tablespoon pesto sauce

8 fully cooked breakfast sausage links, defrosted

DIRECTIONS

1 Preheat the air fryer to 320 degrees.

2 In a medium bowl, crack the eggs and whisk with the pepper, salt, and milk. Pour into a frying pan over medium heat and scramble. Just before the eggs are done, turn off the heat and add in the cheese. Continue to cook until the cheese has melted and the eggs are finished (about 5 minutes total). Remove from the heat.

3 Remove the crescent rolls from the package and press them flat onto a clean surface lightly dusted with flour. Add 1½ teaspoons of pesto sauce across the center of each roll. Place equal portions of eggs across all 8 rolls. Then top each roll with a sausage link and roll the dough up tight so it resembles the crescent-roll shape.

4 Lightly spray your air fryer basket with olive oil mist and place the rolls on top. Bake for 6 minutes or until the tops of the rolls are lightly browned.

5 Remove and let cool 3 to 5 minutes before serving.

NOTE: The rolls will keep in an airtight container in the refrigerator for 2 to 3 days.

TIP: To reheat, use the air fryer to get that crispy, crunchy consistency.

VARY IT! Prefer to go vegetarian? Nix the sausage and add finely chopped vegetables to the scrambled eggs instead.

Mediterranean Egg Sandwich

PREP TIME: 3 MIN | COOK TIME: 8 MIN | YIELD: 1 SANDWICH

INGREDIENTS

1 large egg

5 baby spinach leaves, chopped

1 tablespoon roasted bell pepper, chopped

1 English muffin

1 thin slice prosciutto or Canadian bacon

DIRECTIONS

1 Spray a ramekin with cooking spray or brush the inside with extra-virgin olive oil.

2 In a small bowl, whisk together the egg, baby spinach, and bell pepper.

3 Split the English muffin in half and spray the inside lightly with cooking spray or brush with extra-virgin olive oil.

4 Preheat the air fryer to 350 degrees for 2 minutes. Place the egg ramekin and open English muffin into the air fryer basket, and cook at 350 degrees for 5 minutes. Open the air fryer drawer and add the prosciutto or bacon; cook for an additional 1 minute.

5 To assemble the sandwich, place the egg on one half of the English muffin, top with prosciutto or bacon, and place the remaining piece of English muffin on top.

NOTE: Prosciutto is salty, so be sure to stick with just a thin slice and adjust the seasonings afterward, if needed.

NOTE: If you don't have a ramekin, a silicone muffin cup can work just as well.

VARY IT! Keep it simple with Canadian bacon and a simple egg, or kick it up a notch with bacon and pepper jack cheese.

French Toast Sticks

PREP TIME: 15 MIN | COOK TIME: 8 MIN | YIELD: 4 SERVINGS

INGREDIENTS

2 eggs

¼ cup half-and-half

½ teaspoon vanilla extract

6 slices wheat bread, cut into 1-inch strips

1 teaspoon ground cinnamon

2 tablespoons granulated sugar

Maple syrup or pureed strawberries for serving

DIRECTIONS

1 In an 8-x-12-inch casserole dish, whisk together the eggs, half-and-half, and vanilla. Lay the strips of bread into the baking dish and flip around. Allow the bread to soak up the egg mixture for 10 minutes.

2 Meanwhile, in a small bowl, stir together the cinnamon and sugar.

3 Place the soaked bread strips into the air fryer basket, not touching one another. Spray with cooking spray and sprinkle the cinnamon and sugar mixture onto the bread sticks.

4 Air fry the French toast sticks at 370 degrees for 8 minutes. Cook in batches, as needed.

5 Serve with maple syrup or pureed strawberries.

NOTE: Depending on the size of your air fryer, you may need to do multiple batches.

VARY IT! Add orange zest and cardamom. Or keep it fun for the kids and blend fresh or frozen fruits for a rainbow of dips.

Pigs in a Blanket

PREP TIME: 20 MIN | COOK TIME: 8 MIN | YIELD: 10 SERVINGS

INGREDIENTS

1 cup all-purpose flour, plus more for rolling

1 teaspoon baking powder

¼ cup salted butter, cut into small pieces

½ cup buttermilk

10 fully cooked breakfast sausage links

DIRECTIONS

1 In a large mixing bowl, whisk together the flour and baking powder. Using your fingers or a pastry blender, cut in the butter until you have small pea-size crumbles.

2 Using a rubber spatula, make a well in the center of the flour mixture. Pour the buttermilk into the well, and fold the mixture together until you form a dough ball.

3 Place the sticky dough onto a floured surface and, using a floured rolling pin, roll out until ½-inch thick. Using a round biscuit cutter, cut out 10 rounds, reshaping the dough and rolling out, as needed.

4 Place 1 fully cooked breakfast sausage link on the left edge of each biscuit and roll up, leaving the ends slightly exposed.

5 Using a pastry brush, brush the biscuits with the whisked eggs, and spray them with cooking spray.

6 Place the pigs in a blanket into the air fryer basket with at least 1 inch between each biscuit. Set the air fryer to 340 degrees and cook for 8 minutes.

NOTE: Don't have buttermilk? No worries! Add 1 teaspoon lemon juice or white vinegar to a liquid measuring cup and fill to the ½ cup mark with milk, stir, and you're ready to use as buttermilk.

TIP: Depending on the size of your air fryer, you may need to do more batches.

VARY IT! No sausage on hand? Opt for ham and cheese instead. For a vegetarian alternative, use vegetarian sausage links instead of traditional sausage links.

Almond Cranberry Granola

PREP TIME: 10 MIN	COOK TIME: 9 MIN	YIELD: 12 SERVINGS

INGREDIENTS

2 tablespoons sesame seeds

¼ cup chopped almonds

¼ cup sunflower seeds

½ cup unsweetened shredded coconut

2 tablespoons unsalted butter, melted or at least softened

2 tablespoons coconut oil

⅓ cup honey

2½ cups oats

¼ teaspoon sea salt

½ cup dried cranberries

DIRECTIONS

1 In a large mixing bowl, stir together the sesame seeds, almonds, sunflower seeds, coconut, butter, coconut oil, honey, oats, and salt.

2 Line the air fryer basket with parchment paper. Punch 8 to 10 holes into the parchment paper with a fork so air can circulate. Pour the granola mixture onto the parchment paper.

3 Air fry the granola at 350 degrees for 9 minutes, stirring every 3 minutes.

4 When cooking is complete, stir in the dried cranberries and allow the mixture to cool. Store in an airtight container up to 2 weeks or freeze for 6 months.

TIP: The trick to keeping dried fruit chewy is to add it after baking.

VARY IT! Use dried cherries and apricots instead of coconut and cranberries, if you like.

Apple Fritters

INGREDIENTS

1 cup all-purpose flour

1½ teaspoons baking powder

¼ teaspoon salt

2 tablespoon brown sugar

1 teaspoon vanilla extract

¾ cup plain Greek yogurt

1 tablespoon cinnamon

1 large Granny Smith apple, cored, peeled, and finely chopped

¼ cup chopped walnuts

½ cup powdered sugar

1 tablespoon milk

DIRECTIONS

1 Preheat the air fryer to 320 degrees.

2 In a medium bowl, combine the flour, baking powder, and salt.

3 In a large bowl, add the brown sugar, vanilla, yogurt, cinnamon, apples, and walnuts. Mix the dry ingredients into the wet, using your hands to combine, until all the ingredients are mixed together. Knead the mixture in the bowl about 4 times.

4 Lightly spray the air fryer basket with olive oil spray.

5 Divide the batter into 6 equally sized balls; then lightly flatten them and place inside the basket. Repeat until all the fritters are formed.

6 Place the basket in the air fryer and cook for 6 minutes, flip, and then cook another 6 minutes.

7 While the fritters are cooking, in a small bowl, mix the powdered sugar with the milk. Set aside.

8 When the cooking completes, remove the air fryer basket and allow the fritters to cool on a wire rack. Drizzle with the homemade glaze and serve.

NOTE: Some air fryers get hotter than others. If your air fryer isn't as hot, increase the temperature to 350 degrees and cook as directed.

TIP: Make ahead of time and wrap in a nice gift box to deliver for a fun treat!

VARY IT! You can use peaches instead of apples and pecans instead of walnuts for a Peach Pecan Fritter!

Cinnamon Sugar Donut Holes

PREP TIME: 1 HR 5 MIN	COOK TIME: 6 MIN	YIELD: 12 SERVINGS

INGREDIENTS

1 cup all-purpose flour

6 tablespoons cane sugar, divided

1 teaspoon baking powder

3 teaspoons ground cinnamon, divided

¼ teaspoon salt

1 large egg

1 teaspoon vanilla extract

2 tablespoons melted butter

DIRECTIONS

1 Preheat the air fryer to 370 degrees.

2 In a small bowl, combine the flour, 2 tablespoons of the sugar, the baking powder, 1 teaspoon of the cinnamon, and the salt. Mix well.

3 In a larger bowl, whisk together the egg, vanilla extract, and butter.

4 Slowly add the dry ingredients into the wet until all the ingredients are uniformly combined. Set the bowl inside the refrigerator for at least 30 minutes.

5 Before you're ready to cook, in a small bowl, mix together the remaining 4 tablespoons of sugar and 2 teaspoons of cinnamon.

6 Liberally spray the air fryer basket with olive oil mist so the donut holes don't stick to the bottom. *Note:* You do *not* want to use parchment paper in this recipe; it may burn if your air fryer is hotter than others.

7 Remove the dough from the refrigerator and divide it into 12 equal donut holes. You can use a 1-ounce serving scoop if you have one.

(continued)

8 Roll each donut hole in the sugar and cinnamon mixture; then place in the air fryer basket. Repeat until all the donut holes are covered in the sugar and cinnamon mixture.

9 When the basket is full, cook for 6 minutes. Remove the donut holes from the basket using oven-safe tongs and let cool 5 minutes. Repeat until all 12 are cooked.

NOTE: Depending on the size of your air fryer basket, you may need to bake the donut holes in two batches. You want to have space around each side of the donut hole to allow it to fully cook.

NOTE: If you want to make the dough ahead of time, you can place it in an airtight container and store it in the refrigerator overnight.

TIP: The donut holes will keep in an airtight container on the counter for 3 days.

VARY IT! Use powdered sugar to coat the outside of the donut holes, or swap in your preferred seasonal spice (like pumpkin pie spice) to give them a holiday twist.

Coffee Cake

PREP TIME: 10 MIN	COOK TIME: 35 MIN	YIELD: 8 SERVINGS

INGREDIENTS

4 tablespoons butter, melted and divided

⅓ cup cane sugar

¼ cup brown sugar

1 large egg

1 cup plus 6 teaspoons milk, divided

1 teaspoon vanilla extract

2 cups all-purpose flour

1½ teaspoons baking powder

¼ teaspoon salt

2 teaspoons ground cinnamon

⅓ cup chopped pecans

⅓ cup powdered sugar

DIRECTIONS

1 Preheat the air fryer to 325 degrees.

2 Using a hand mixer or stand mixer, in a medium bowl, cream together the butter, cane sugar, brown sugar, the egg, 1 cup of the milk, and the vanilla. Set aside.

3 In a small bowl, mix together the flour, baking powder, salt, and cinnamon. Slowly combine the dry ingredients into the wet. Fold in the pecans.

4 Liberally spray a 7-inch springform pan with cooking spray. Pour the batter into the pan and place in the air fryer basket.

5 Bake for 30 to 35 minutes. While the cake is baking, in a small bowl, add the powdered sugar and whisk together with the remaining 6 teaspoons of milk. Set aside.

6 When the cake is done baking, remove the pan from the basket and let cool on a wire rack. After 10 minutes, remove and invert the cake from pan. Drizzle with the powdered sugar glaze and serve.

NOTE: The cake will keep in an airtight container on the counter for 3 days or in the fridge for about a week.

TIP: Have an oven-safe Bundt cake pan that will fit in your air fryer basket? Try using that to create a fun, bakery-like feel!

VARY IT! Add in chocolate chips, dried raisins, or your favorite nut.

Chapter **6**

Bread Basics

W ho doesn't love the smell of freshly baked bread? We sure do, and we're hoping you feel the same way!

To help show you how you can make some of the most basic breads in your air fryer, we've tested out our favorites. From muffins to scones, bagels and breads, rolls and naan, there's something for everyone in this chapter.

WARNING

You can make most of these breads using gluten-free flours, but some of the properties that make these basic breads so delicious revolve around the gluten in the flours we've used. So, although we encourage you to try these out with whatever gluten-free flour you prefer, we recommend you start with smaller batches until you get the right combination of ingredients that work best for you.

TIP

We found variations among various brands of air fryers during the testing process. Some brands run hotter than others, so when baking it's important to watch the bread closely. Consider checking for doneness sooner than the recipes in this chapter instruct, especially if you know your machine runs hotter.

Chocolate Chip Banana Muffins

PREP TIME: 10 MIN	COOK TIME: 14 MIN	YIELD: 12 SERVINGS

INGREDIENTS

2 medium bananas, mashed

¼ cup brown sugar

1½ teaspoons vanilla extract

⅔ cup milk

2 tablespoons butter

1 large egg

1 cup white whole-wheat flour

½ cup old-fashioned oats

1 teaspoon baking soda

½ teaspoon baking powder

⅛ teaspoon sea salt

¼ cup mini chocolate chips

DIRECTIONS

1 Preheat the air fryer to 330 degrees.

2 In a large bowl, combine the bananas, brown sugar, vanilla extract, milk, butter, and egg; set aside.

3 In a separate bowl, combine the flour, oats, baking soda, baking powder, and salt.

4 Slowly add the dry ingredients into the wet ingredients, folding in the flour mixture ⅓ cup at a time.

5 Mix in the chocolate chips and set aside.

6 Using silicone muffin liners, fill 6 muffin liners two-thirds full. Carefully place the muffin liners in the air fryer basket and bake for 20 minutes (or until the tops are browned and a toothpick inserted in the center comes out clean). Carefully remove the muffins from the basket and repeat with the remaining batter.

7 Serve warm.

NOTE: Store in an airtight container on the counter for up to 5 days, in the refrigerator for up to 1 week, or in the freezer for 3 months.

Strawberry Streusel Muffins

PREP TIME: 10 MIN | COOK TIME: 14 MIN | YIELD: 12 SERVINGS

INGREDIENTS

1¾ cups all-purpose flour

½ cup granulated sugar

2 teaspoons baking powder

¼ teaspoon baking soda

½ teaspoon salt

½ cup plain yogurt

½ cup milk

¼ cup vegetable oil

2 large eggs

1 teaspoon vanilla extract

½ cup freeze-dried strawberries

2 tablespoons brown sugar

¼ cup oats

2 tablespoons butter

DIRECTIONS

1 Preheat the air fryer to 330 degrees.

2 In a large bowl, whisk together the flour, sugar, baking powder, baking soda, and salt; set aside.

3 In a separate bowl, whisk together the yogurt, milk, vegetable oil, eggs, and vanilla extract.

4 Make a well in the dry ingredients; then pour the wet ingredients into the well of the dry ingredients. Using a rubber spatula, mix the ingredients for 1 minute or until slightly lumpy. Fold in the strawberries.

5 In a small bowl, use your fingers to mix together the brown sugar, oats, and butter until coarse crumbles appear. Divide the mixture in half.

6 Using silicone muffin liners, fill 6 muffin liners two-thirds full.

7 Crumble half of the streusel topping onto the first batch of muffins.

8 Carefully place the muffin liners in the air fryer basket and bake for 14 minutes (or until the tops are browned and a toothpick inserted in the center comes out clean). Carefully remove the muffins from the basket and repeat with the remaining batter and topping.

9 Serve warm.

NOTE: Store in an airtight container on the counter for up to 3 days, in the refrigerator for up to 5 days, or in the freezer for 3 months.

NOTE: This is a good basic muffin recipe. By using freeze-dried strawberries you're not adding any liquid to the mix. If you use fresh or frozen strawberries, you'll need to add more flour.

VARY IT! Any dried fruit will work well in this recipe. Try dried cherries with orange zest or dried blueberries.

Carrot Orange Muffins

PREP TIME: 10 MIN	COOK TIME: 12 MIN	YIELD: 12 SERVINGS

INGREDIENTS

1½ cups all-purpose flour

½ cup granulated sugar

½ teaspoon ground cinnamon

2 teaspoons baking powder

¼ teaspoon baking soda

½ teaspoon salt

2 large eggs

¼ cup vegetable oil

⅓ cup orange marmalade

2 cups grated carrots

DIRECTIONS

1 Preheat the air fryer to 320 degrees.

2 In a large bowl, whisk together the flour, sugar, cinnamon, baking powder, baking soda, and salt; set aside.

3 In a separate bowl, whisk together the eggs, vegetable oil, orange marmalade, and grated carrots.

4 Make a well in the dry ingredients; then pour the wet ingredients into the well of the dry ingredients. Using a rubber spatula, mix the ingredients for 1 minute or until slightly lumpy.

5 Using silicone muffin liners, fill 6 muffin liners two-thirds full.

6 Carefully place the muffin liners in the air fryer basket and bake for 12 minutes (or until the tops are browned and a toothpick inserted in the center comes out clean). Carefully remove the muffins from the basket and repeat with remaining batter.

7 Serve warm.

NOTE: Store in an airtight container on the counter for up to 5 days, in the refrigerator for up to 1 week, or in the freezer for 3 months.

TIP: You can use glass ramekins or 6-ounce Mason jars instead of silicone muffin cups. Just be sure to not let the ramekins or jars touch one another.

VARY IT! Spice up this recipe with a dash of ground ginger. Craving a crunch? Add chopped almonds, walnuts, or pecans.

English Scones

PREP TIME: 15 MIN | COOK TIME: 8 MIN | YIELD: 8 SERVINGS

INGREDIENTS

2 cups all-purpose flour

1 tablespoon baking powder

½ teaspoon salt

2 tablespoons sugar

¼ cup unsalted butter

⅔ cup plus 1 tablespoon whole milk, divided

DIRECTIONS

1 Preheat the air fryer to 380 degrees.

2 In a large bowl, whisk together the flour, baking powder, salt, and sugar. Using a pastry blender or your fingers, cut in the butter until pea-size crumbles appear. Make a well in the center and pour in ⅔ cup of the milk. Quickly mix the batter until a ball forms. Knead the dough 3 times.

3 Place the dough onto a floured surface and, using your hands or a rolling pin, flatten the dough until it's ¾ inch thick. Using a biscuit cutter or drinking glass, cut out 10 circles, reforming the dough and flattening as needed to use up the batter.

4 Brush the tops lightly with the remaining 1 tablespoon of milk.

5 Place the scones into the air fryer basket. Cook for 8 minutes or until golden brown and cooked in the center.

NOTE: Store in an airtight container on the counter for up to 3 days or in the freezer for 3 months.

TIP: Keep things cold! From the flour to the butter to the milk, the colder everything is, the better the scones will turn out.

TIP: Serve with fresh jam and whipped honey butter. Or go savory with cream cheese and chives.

VARY IT! Add in ½ cup fresh blueberries and lemon zest for berry scones. Or try a savory scone with cheddar cheese.

Sweet and Spicy Pumpkin Scones

PREP TIME: 12 MIN	COOK TIME: 8 MIN	YIELD: 8 SERVINGS

INGREDIENTS

2 cups all-purpose flour

3 tablespoons packed brown sugar

½ teaspoon baking powder

¼ teaspoon baking soda

½ teaspoon kosher salt

½ teaspoon ground cinnamon

¼ teaspoon ground ginger

¼ teaspoon ground cardamom

4 tablespoons cold unsalted butter

½ cup plus 2 tablespoons pumpkin puree, divided

4 tablespoons milk, divided

1 large egg

1 cup powdered sugar

DIRECTIONS

1   In a large bowl, mix together the flour, brown sugar, baking powder, baking soda, salt, cinnamon, ginger, and cardamom. Using a pastry blender or two knives, cut in the butter until coarse crumbles appear.

2   In a small bowl, whisk together ½ cup of the pumpkin puree, 2 tablespoons of the milk, and the egg until combined. Pour the wet ingredients into the dry ingredients; stir to combine.

3   Form the dough into a ball and place onto a floured service. Press the dough out or use a rolling pin to roll out the dough until ½ inch thick and in a circle. Cut the dough into 8 wedges.

4   Bake at 360 degrees for 8 to 10 minutes or until completely cooked through. Cook in batches as needed.

5   In a medium bowl, whisk together the powdered sugar, the remaining 2 tablespoons of pumpkin puree, and the remaining 2 tablespoons of milk. When the pumpkin scones have cooled, drizzle the pumpkin glaze over the top before serving.

NOTE: Store without glaze in an airtight container on the counter for up to 5 days, in the refrigerator for up to 1 week, or in the freezer for 3 months. To reheat the scones straight from the freezer, preheat your oven to 340 degrees and bake for 12 minutes.

VARY IT! Add in chopped pecans or top with pumpkin seeds for a festive touch.

Mini Everything Bagels

PREP TIME: 10 MIN | **COOK TIME: 6 MIN** | **YIELD: 4 SERVINGS**

INGREDIENTS

1 cup all-purpose flour

2 teaspoons baking powder

½ teaspoon salt

1 cup plain Greek yogurt

1 egg, whisked

1 teaspoon sesame seeds

1 teaspoon dehydrated onions

½ teaspoon poppy seeds

½ teaspoon garlic powder

½ teaspoon sea salt flakes

DIRECTIONS

1 In a large bowl, mix together the flour, baking powder, and salt. Make a well in the dough and add in the Greek yogurt. Mix with a spoon until a dough forms.

2 Place the dough onto a heavily floured surface and knead for 3 minutes. You may use up to 1 cup of additional flour as you knead the dough, if necessary.

3 Cut the dough into 8 pieces and roll each piece into a 6-inch, snakelike piece. Touch the ends of each piece together so it closes the circle and forms a bagel shape. Brush the tops of the bagels with the whisked egg.

4 In a small bowl, combine the sesame seeds, dehydrated onions, poppy seeds, garlic powder, and sea salt flakes. Sprinkle the seasoning on top of the bagels.

5 Preheat the air fryer to 360 degrees. Using a bench scraper or flat-edged spatula, carefully place the bagels into the air fryer basket. Spray the bagel tops with cooking spray. Air-fry the bagels for 6 minutes or until golden brown. Allow the bread to cool at least 10 minutes before slicing for serving.

NOTE: Store in an airtight container on the counter for up to 2 days.

NOTE: Depending on the size of your air fryer, you may need to do 2 or 3 batches.

TIP: Keep your hands and surface heavily floured while kneading the dough. The dough should not stick to your hands when it's ready to roll out.

VARY IT! Craving something sweet? Knead in raisins and top with cinnamon and sugar instead. Also, if you want to up the fiber and nutrients content, you can use whole-wheat pastry flour instead of all-purpose flour.

Wild Blueberry Lemon Chia Bread

PREP TIME: 10 MIN	COOK TIME: 27 MIN	YIELD: 6 SERVINGS

INGREDIENTS

¼ cup extra-virgin olive oil

⅓ cup plus 1 tablespoon cane sugar

1 large egg

3 tablespoons fresh lemon juice

1 tablespoon lemon zest

⅔ cup milk

1 cup all-purpose flour

¾ teaspoon baking powder

⅛ teaspoon salt

2 tablespoons chia seeds

1 cup frozen wild blueberries

⅓ cup powdered sugar

2 teaspoons milk

DIRECTIONS

1 Preheat the air fryer to 310 degrees.

2 In a medium bowl, mix the olive oil with the sugar. Whisk in the egg, lemon juice, lemon zest, and milk; set aside.

3 In a small bowl, combine the all-purpose flour, baking powder, and salt.

4 Slowly mix the dry ingredients into the wet ingredients. Stir in the chia seeds and wild blueberries.

5 Liberally spray a 7-inch springform pan with olive-oil spray. Pour the batter into the pan and place the pan in the air fryer. Bake for 25 to 27 minutes, or until a toothpick inserted in the center comes out clean.

6 Remove and let cool on a wire rack for 10 minutes prior to removing from the pan.

7 Meanwhile, in a small bowl, mix the powdered sugar with the milk to create the glaze.

8 Slice and serve with a drizzle of the powdered sugar glaze.

NOTE: Store in an airtight container in the refrigerator for up to 1 week or in the freezer for up to 3 months.

NOTE: For a healthier bread with more fiber, swap white whole wheat flour for all-purpose.

TIP: Wild blueberries are smaller than conventional. You can find them in the frozen fruit section of your local market.

Zucchini Walnut Bread

PREP TIME: 10 MIN	COOK TIME: 30 MIN	YIELD: 6 SERVINGS

INGREDIENTS

¾ cup all-purpose flour

½ teaspoon baking soda

1 teaspoon ground cinnamon

⅛ teaspoon salt

1 large egg

⅓ cup packed brown sugar

¼ cup canola oil

1 teaspoon vanilla extract

⅓ cup milk

1 medium zucchini, shredded (about 1⅓ cups)

⅓ cup chopped walnuts

DIRECTIONS

1 Preheat the air fryer to 320 degrees.

2 In a medium bowl, mix together the flour, baking soda, cinnamon, and salt.

3 In a large bowl, whisk together the egg, brown sugar, oil, vanilla, and milk. Stir in the zucchini.

4 Slowly fold the dry ingredients into the wet ingredients. Stir in the chopped walnuts. Then pour the batter into two 4-inch oven-safe loaf pans.

5 Bake for 30 minutes or until a toothpick inserted into the center comes out clean. Let cool before slicing.

NOTE: Store tightly wrapped on the counter for up to 5 days, in the refrigerator for up to 10 days, or in the freezer for 3 months.

TIP: For a healthier bread with more fiber, use white whole-wheat flour instead of all-purpose flour.

VARY IT! Like a chocolaty taste? Mix in ⅓ cup chocolate chips!

Classic Cinnamon Rolls

PREP TIME: 10 MIN	COOK TIME: 6 MIN	YIELD: 4 SERVINGS

INGREDIENTS

1½ cups all-purpose flour

1 tablespoon granulated sugar

2 teaspoons baking powder

½ teaspoon salt

4 tablespoons butter, divided

½ cup buttermilk

2 tablespoons brown sugar

1 teaspoon cinnamon

1 cup powdered sugar

2 tablespoons milk

DIRECTIONS

1 Preheat the air fryer to 360 degrees.

2 In a large bowl, stir together the flour, sugar, baking powder, and salt. Cut in 3 tablespoons of the butter with a pastry blender or two knives until coarse crumbs remain. Stir in the buttermilk until a dough forms.

3 Place the dough onto a floured surface and roll out into a square shape about ½ inch thick.

4 Melt the remaining 1 tablespoon of butter in the microwave for 20 seconds. Using a pastry brush or your fingers, spread the melted butter onto the dough.

5 In a small bowl, mix together the brown sugar and cinnamon. Sprinkle the mixture across the surface of the dough. Roll the dough up, forming a long log. Using a pastry cutter or sharp knife, cut 10 cinnamon rolls.

6 Carefully place the cinnamon rolls into the air fryer basket. Then bake at 360 degrees for 6 minutes or until golden brown.

7 Meanwhile, in a small bowl, whisk together the powdered sugar and milk.

8 Plate the cinnamon rolls and drizzle the glaze over the surface before serving.

NOTE: Store without glaze in an airtight container on the counter for up to 3 days, in the refrigerator for up to 1 week, or in the freezer for 3 months.

VARY IT! Add in chopped pecans or walnuts for a little crunch.

Parmesan Garlic Naan

PREP TIME: 10 MIN | **COOK TIME: 4 MIN** | **YIELD: 6 SERVINGS**

INGREDIENTS

1 cup bread flour

1 teaspoon baking powder

⅛ teaspoon salt

1 teaspoon garlic powder

2 tablespoon shredded parmesan cheese

1 cup plain 2% fat Greek yogurt

1 tablespoon extra-virgin olive oil

DIRECTIONS

1 Preheat the air fryer to 400 degrees.

2 In a medium bowl, mix the flour, baking powder, salt, garlic powder, and cheese. Mix the yogurt into the flour, using your hands to combine if necessary.

3 On a flat surface covered with flour, divide the dough into 6 equal balls and roll each out into a 4-inch-diameter circle.

4 Lightly brush both sides of each naan with olive oil and place one naan at a time into the basket. Cook for 3 to 4 minutes (or until the bread begins to rise and brown on the outside). Remove and repeat for the remaining breads.

5 Serve warm.

NOTE: Store in an airtight container in the refrigerator for up to 1 week.

TIP: Reheat the naan in the air fryer for 2 minutes at 400 degrees.

VARY IT! Add in your favorite cheese or spices to create your own flavor. Mozzarella cheese, basil, and sundried tomatoes make a fun pizza naan flavor.

Green Onion Pancakes

PREP TIME: 45 MIN   COOK TIME: 8 MIN   YIELD: 4 SERVINGS

INGREDIENTS

2 cup all-purpose flour

½ teaspoon salt

¾ cup hot water

1 tablespoon vegetable oil

1 tablespoon butter, melted

2 cups finely chopped green onions

1 tablespoon black sesame seeds, for garnish

DIRECTIONS

1 In a large bowl, whisk together the flour and salt. Make a well in the center and pour in the hot water. Quickly stir the flour mixture together until a dough forms. Knead the dough for 5 minutes; then cover with a warm, wet towel and set aside for 30 minutes to rest.

2 In a small bowl, mix together the vegetable oil and melted butter.

3 On a floured surface, place the dough and cut it into 8 pieces. Working with 1 piece of dough at a time, use a rolling pin to roll out the dough until it's ¼ inch thick; then brush the surface with the oil and butter mixture and sprinkle with green onions. Next, fold the dough in half and then in half again. Roll out the dough again until it's ¼ inch thick and brush with the oil and butter mixture and green onions. Fold the dough in half and then in half again and roll out one last time until it's ¼ inch thick. Repeat this technique with all 8 pieces.

4 Meanwhile, preheat the air fryer to 400 degrees.

5 Place 1 or 2 pancakes into the air fryer basket (or as many as will fit in your fryer), and cook for 2 minutes or until crispy and golden brown. Repeat until all the pancakes are cooked. Top with black sesame seeds for garnish, if desired.

NOTE: Green onion pancakes are a savory bread commonly served with Asian cuisine, but these go great with fried chicken, too!

TIP: Serve with a soy dipping sauce: 3 tablespoons soy sauce, 2 tablespoons lime juice, 2 teaspoons sesame oil, ¼ cup vegetable oil, and 1 tablespoon sesame seeds. Whisk together and serve as a dip.

VARY IT! Don't have green onions? Use chopped shallots or garlic instead.

Chapter 7

Starters

Tired of feeling like the only appetizer you make is a cheese tray? We aren't knocking that — we both love our cheese — but we've found that using our air fryer to create delicious, nutritious, and crowd-pleasing appetizers is a lot easier than we imagined!

Egg rolls? Wontons? Tater-tots? All of these are totally attainable, and they don't require a culinary degree to make them come to life!

We've taken some of our dining-out favorites and turned them into easy-to-make, do-it-yourself appetizers. Who's ready for a party? We sure are!

Avocado Fries

PREP TIME: 15 MIN	COOK TIME: 8 MIN	YIELD: 8 SERVINGS

INGREDIENTS

2 medium avocados, firm but ripe

1 large egg

½ teaspoon garlic powder

¼ teaspoon cayenne pepper

¼ teaspoon salt

¾ cup almond flour

½ cup finely grated Parmesan cheese

½ cup gluten-free breadcrumbs

DIRECTIONS

1 Preheat the air fryer to 370 degrees.

2 Rinse the outside of the avocado with water. Slice the avocado in half, slice it in half again, and then slice it in half once more to get 8 slices. Remove the outer skin. Repeat for the other avocado. Set the avocado slices aside.

3 In a small bowl, whisk the egg, garlic powder, cayenne pepper, and salt in a small bowl. Set aside.

4 In a separate bowl, pour the almond flour.

5 In a third bowl, mix the Parmesan cheese and breadcrumbs.

6 Carefully roll the avocado slices in the almond flour, then dip them in the egg wash, and coat them in the cheese and bread-crumb topping. Repeat until all 16 fries are coated.

7 Liberally spray the air fryer basket with olive oil spray and place the avocado fries into the basket, leaving a little space around the sides between fries. Depending on the size of your air fryer, you may need to cook these in batches.

8 Cook fries for 8 minutes, or until the outer coating turns light brown.

9 Carefully remove, repeat with remaining slices, and then serve warm.

NOTE: These fries are gluten-free, but you can use an all-purpose flour and traditional breadcrumb or panko coating if gluten-free isn't a necessity for you.

TIP: Serve with your favorite sauce. A yogurt-based ranch tastes great, as does a spicy sriracha!

Avocado Egg Rolls

PREP TIME: 20 MIN	COOK TIME: 8 MIN	YIELD: 8 SERVINGS

INGREDIENTS

8 full-size egg roll wrappers

1 medium avocado, sliced into 8 pieces

1 cup cooked black beans, divided

½ cup mild salsa, divided

½ cup shredded Mexican cheese, divided

⅓ cup filtered water, divided

½ cup sour cream

1 teaspoon chipotle hot sauce

DIRECTIONS

1 Preheat the air fryer to 400 degrees.

2 Place the egg roll wrapper on a flat surface and place 1 strip of avocado down in the center.

3 Top the avocado with 2 tablespoons of black beans, 1 tablespoon of salsa, and 1 tablespoon of shredded cheese.

4 Place two of your fingers into the water, and then moisten the four outside edges of the egg roll wrapper with water (so the outer edges will secure shut).

5 Fold the bottom corner up, covering the filling. Then secure the sides over the top, remembering to lightly moisten them so they stick. Tightly roll the egg roll up and moisten the final flap of the wrapper and firmly press it into the egg roll to secure it shut.

6 Repeat Steps 2–5 until all 8 egg rolls are complete.

7 When ready to cook, spray the air fryer basket with olive oil spray and place the egg rolls into the basket. Depending on the size and type of air fryer you have, you may need to do this in two sets.

8 Cook for 4 minutes, flip, and then cook the remaining 4 minutes.

9 Repeat until all the egg rolls are cooked. Meanwhile, mix the sour cream with the hot sauce to serve as a dipping sauce.

10 Serve warm.

NOTE: You can scale this recipe up or down depending on how many you're cooking for.

TIP: Slice the egg rolls in half, top with chopped cilantro, and serve on a platter with a spicy green sauce and sour cream salsa for a great presentation.

VARY IT! Prefer a different filling? Go for it! Thai spiced ground chicken with cabbage tastes great with a peanut dipping sauce, too!

Tempura Fried Veggies

PREP TIME: 15 MIN	COOK TIME: 6 MIN	YIELD: 4 SERVINGS

INGREDIENTS

½ cup all-purpose flour

½ teaspoon black pepper

¼ teaspoon salt

2 large eggs

1¼ cups panko breadcrumbs

1 tablespoon extra-virgin olive oil

1 cup white button mushrooms, cleaned

1 medium zucchini, skinned and sliced

1 medium carrot, skinned sliced

DIRECTIONS

1 Preheat the air fryer to 400 degrees.

2 In a small bowl, mix the flour, pepper, and salt.

3 In a separate bowl, whisk the eggs.

4 In a third bowl, mix together the breadcrumbs and olive oil.

5 Begin to batter the vegetables by placing them one at a time into the flour, then dipping them in the eggs, and coating them in breadcrumbs. When you've prepared enough to begin air frying, liberally spray the air fryer basket with olive oil and place the vegetables inside.

6 Cook for 6 minutes, or until the breadcrumb coating on the outside appears golden brown. Repeat coating the other vegetables while the first batch is cooking.

7 When the cooking completes, carefully remove the vegetables and keep them warm. Repeat cooking for the remaining vegetables until all are cooked.

8 Serve warm.

NOTE: These vegetables are best served immediately. You can reheat them in the air fryer if you store them in the refrigerator, but they don't taste nearly as good.

TIP: Make this recipe gluten-free by using gluten-free flour and breadcrumbs to coat the vegetables.

TIP: Keep the vegetables warm by enlisting the help of your oven. Set it to 200 degrees and place the cooked tempura vegetables on a baking sheet and place them in the oven until all have been air fried.

VARY IT! Use whatever spices you like to season the flour, and use whatever vegetables you enjoy or have on hand.

Herbed Cheese Brittle

PREP TIME: 10 MIN | COOK TIME: 5 MIN | YIELD: 4 SERVINGS

INGREDIENTS

½ cup shredded Parmesan cheese

½ cup shredded white cheddar cheese

1 tablespoon fresh chopped rosemary

1 teaspoon garlic powder

1 large egg white

DIRECTIONS

1 Preheat the air fryer to 400 degrees.

2 In a large bowl, mix the cheeses, rosemary, and garlic powder. Mix in the egg white. Then pour the batter into a 7-inch pan (or an air-fryer-compatible pan). Place the pan in the air fryer basket and cook for 4 to 5 minutes, or until the cheese is melted and slightly browned.

3 Remove the pan from the air fryer, and let it cool for 2 minutes. Invert the pan before the cheese brittle completely cools but is semi-hardened to allow it to easily slide out of the pan.

4 Let the pan cool another 5 minutes. Break into pieces and serve.

TIP: If you don't have fresh herbs, feel free to use dried. Use 1 teaspoon of dried herbs for every 1 tablespoon of fresh.

VARY IT! Use your preferred cheeses and herbs to make this recipe your own. You can even add small pieces of pepperoni to make it a cheese pepperoni brittle.

Za'atar Garbanzo Beans

| PREP TIME: 5 MIN | COOK TIME: 12 MIN | YIELD: 6 SERVINGS |

INGREDIENTS

One 14.5-ounce can garbanzo beans, drained and rinsed

1 tablespoon extra-virgin olive oil

6 teaspoons za'atar seasoning mix

2 tablespoons chopped parsley

Salt and pepper, to taste

DIRECTIONS

1 Preheat the air fryer to 390 degrees.

2 In a medium bowl, toss the garbanzo beans with olive oil and za'atar seasoning.

3 Pour the beans into the air fryer basket and cook for 12 to 15 minutes, or until toasted as you like. Stir every 3 minutes while roasting.

4 Remove the beans from the air fryer basket into a serving bowl, top with fresh chopped parsley, and season with salt and pepper.

NOTE: See Chapter 2 to make your own za'atar seasoning mix if you can't find it at your local market.

VARY IT! If you prefer a Cajun seasoning or an Indian seasoning, you can simply replace the za'atar with your preferred spice mixture. Another favorite is ranch-flavored toasted garbanzo beans.

Buffalo Cauliflower

INGREDIENTS

1 large head of cauliflower, washed and cut into medium-size florets

½ cup all-purpose flour

¼ cup melted butter

3 tablespoons hot sauce

½ teaspoon garlic powder

½ cup blue cheese dip or ranch dressing (optional)

DIRECTIONS

1 Preheat the air fryer to 350 degrees.

2 Make sure the cauliflower florets are dry, and then coat them in flour.

3 Liberally spray the air fryer basket with an olive oil mist. Place the cauliflower into the basket, making sure not to stack them on top of each other. Depending on the size of your air fryer, you may need to do this in two batches.

4 Cook for 6 minutes, then shake the basket, and cook another 6 minutes.

5 While cooking, mix the melted butter, hot sauce, and garlic powder in a large bowl.

6 Carefully remove the cauliflower from the air fryer. Toss the cauliflower into the butter mixture to coat. Repeat Steps 2–4 for any leftover cauliflower. Serve warm with the dip of your choice.

NOTE: To make this recipe gluten free, use a gluten-free flour like almond or cassava.

TIP: For an extra boost of flavor (and additional vitamin B12), mix ¼ cup of nutritional yeast into the flour before coating the cauliflower.

Indian Cauliflower Tikka Bites

PREP TIME: 10 MIN	COOK TIME: 20 MIN	YIELD: 6 SERVINGS

INGREDIENTS

1 cup plain Greek yogurt

1 teaspoon fresh ginger

1 teaspoon minced garlic

1 teaspoon vindaloo

½ teaspoon cardamom

½ teaspoon paprika

½ teaspoon turmeric powder

½ teaspoon cumin powder

1 large head of cauliflower, washed and cut into medium-size florets

½ cup panko breadcrumbs

1 lemon, quartered

DIRECTIONS

1 Preheat the air fryer to 350 degrees.

2 In a large bowl, mix the yogurt, ginger, garlic, vindaloo, cardamom, paprika, turmeric, and cumin. Add the cauliflower florets to the bowl, and coat them with the yogurt.

3 Remove the cauliflower florets from the bowl and place them on a baking sheet. Sprinkle the panko breadcrumbs over the top. Place the cauliflower bites into the air fryer basket, leaving space between the florets. Depending on the size of your air fryer, you may need to make more than one batch.

4 Cook the cauliflower for 10 minutes, shake the basket, and continue cooking another 10 minutes (or until the florets are lightly browned).

5 Remove from the air fryer and keep warm. Continue to cook until all the florets are done.

6 Before serving, lightly squeeze lemon over the top. Serve warm.

TIP: If you don't have vindaloo, you can use garam masala instead. They aren't the same spice, but they both taste great!

Panko-Breaded Onion Rings

PREP TIME: 15 MIN | COOK TIME: 12 MIN | YIELD: 4 SERVINGS

INGREDIENTS

1 large sweet onion, cut into ½-inch slices and rings separated

2 cups ice water

½ cup all-purpose flour

1 teaspoon paprika

1 teaspoon salt

½ teaspoon black pepper

½ teaspoon garlic powder

¼ teaspoon onion powder

1 egg, whisked

2 tablespoons milk

1 cup breadcrumbs

DIRECTIONS

1 Preheat the air fryer to 400 degrees.

2 In a large bowl, soak the onion rings in the water for 5 minutes. Drain and pat dry with a towel.

3 In a medium bowl, place the flour, paprika, salt, pepper, garlic powder, and onion powder.

4 In a second bowl, whisk together the egg and milk.

5 In a third bowl, place the breadcrumbs.

6 To bread the onion rings, dip them first into the flour mixture, then into the egg mixture (shaking off the excess), and then into the breadcrumbs. Place the coated onion rings onto a plate while you bread all the rings.

7 Place the onion rings into the air fryer basket in a single layer, sometimes nesting smaller rings into larger rings. Spray with cooking spray. Cook for 3 minutes, turn the rings over, and spray with more cooking spray. Cook for another 3 to 5 minutes. Cook the rings in batches; you may need to do 2 or 3 batches, depending on the size of your air fryer.

TIP: Serve with a variety of dips, from ranch dressing to ketchup to barbecue sauce.

"Fried" Pickles with Homemade Ranch

PREP TIME: 5 MIN	COOK TIME: 8 MIN	YIELD: 8 SERVINGS

INGREDIENTS

1 cup all-purpose flour

2 teaspoons dried dill

½ teaspoon paprika

¾ cup buttermilk

1 egg

4 large kosher dill pickles, sliced ¼-inch thick

2 cups panko breadcrumbs

DIRECTIONS

1 Preheat the air fryer to 380 degrees.

2 In a medium bowl, whisk together the flour, dill, paprika, buttermilk, and egg.

3 Dip and coat thick slices of dill pickles into the batter. Next, dredge into the panko breadcrumbs.

4 Place a single layer of breaded pickles into the air fryer basket. Spray the pickles with cooking spray. Cook for 4 minutes, turn over, and cook another 4 minutes. Repeat until all the pickle chips have been cooked.

NOTE Some air fryers cook hotter, so adjust the time as needed.

TIP: Serve these pickles with a spicy or classic ranch dressing.

VARY IT! This same batter works well on a variety of vegetables, like summer squash and red bell peppers.

Zucchini Fritters

| PREP TIME: 15 MIN | COOK TIME: 10 MIN | YIELD: 8 SERVINGS |

INGREDIENTS

2 cups grated zucchini

½ teaspoon sea salt

1 egg

½ teaspoon garlic powder

¼ teaspoon onion powder

¼ cup grated Parmesan cheese

½ cup all-purpose flour

¼ teaspoon baking powder

½ cup Greek yogurt or sour cream

½ lime, juiced

¼ cup chopped cilantro

¼ teaspoon ground cumin

¼ teaspoon salt

DIRECTIONS

1 Preheat the air fryer to 360 degrees.

2 In a large colander, place a kitchen towel. Inside the towel, place the grated zucchini and sprinkle the sea salt over the top. Let the zucchini sit for 5 minutes; then, using the towel, squeeze dry the zucchini.

3 In a medium bowl, mix together the egg, garlic powder, onion powder, Parmesan cheese, flour, and baking powder. Add in the grated zucchini, and stir until completely combined.

4 Pierce a piece of parchment paper with a fork 4 to 6 times. Place the parchment paper into the air fryer basket. Using a tablespoon, place 6 to 8 heaping tablespoons of fritter batter onto the parchment paper. Spray the fritters with cooking spray and cook for 5 minutes, turn the fritters over, and cook another 5 minutes.

5 Meanwhile, while the fritters are cooking, make the sauce. In a small bowl, whisk together the Greek yogurt or sour cream, lime juice, cilantro, cumin, and salt.

6 Repeat Steps 2–4 with the remaining batter.

NOTE: This recipe will make 24 to 30 bite-size fritters.

TIP: You can make larger fritters for a main course meal instead.

VARY IT! Try a Mediterranean-inspired dip with Greek yogurt, chopped garlic, lemon zest, lemon juice, and parsley.

Crispy Wontons

PREP TIME: 15 MIN   COOK TIME: 10 MIN   YIELD: 8 SERVINGS

INGREDIENTS

½ cup refried beans

3 tablespoons salsa

¼ cup canned artichoke hearts, drained and patted dry

¼ cup frozen spinach, defrosted and squeezed dry

2 ounces cream cheese

1½ teaspoons dried oregano, divided

¼ teaspoon garlic powder

¼ teaspoon onion powder

½ teaspoon salt

¼ cup chopped pepperoni

¼ cup grated mozzarella cheese

1 tablespoon grated Parmesan

2 ounces cream cheese

½ teaspoon dried oregano

32 wontons

1 cup water

DIRECTIONS

1   Preheat the air fryer to 370 degrees.

2   In a medium bowl, mix together the refried beans and salsa.

3   In a second medium bowl, mix together the artichoke hearts, spinach, cream cheese, oregano, garlic powder, onion powder, and salt.

4   In a third medium bowl, mix together the pepperoni, mozzarella cheese, Parmesan cheese, cream cheese, and the remaining ½ teaspoon of oregano.

5   Get a towel lightly damp with water and ring it out. While working with the wontons, leave the unfilled wontons under the damp towel so they don't dry out.

6   Working with 8 wontons at a time, place 2 teaspoons of one of the fillings into the center of the wonton, rotating among the different fillings (one filling per wonton). Working one at a time, use a pastry brush, dip the pastry brush into the water, and brush the edges of the dough with the water. Fold the dough in half to form a triangle and set aside. Continue until 8 wontons are formed. Spray the wontons with cooking spray and cover with a dry towel. Repeat until all 32 wontons have been filled.

7   Place the wontons into the air fryer basket, leaving space between the wontons, and cook for 5 minutes. Turn over and check for brownness, and then cook for another 5 minutes.

NOTE: This recipe can satisfy a range of guests at a party, from vegetarians to kids. This is also a great recipe to get kids cooking. Let them help from start to finish!

TIP: Serve the wontons filled with refried beans and salsa with a ranch dressing or Mexican crema. Serve the other two varieties of wontons with a marinara dipping sauce.

VARY IT! The sky's the limit with what you fill in wonton wrappers, from something sweet like fruit jam to something savory and meaty. Get creative and have fun!

Loaded Potato Skins

PREP TIME: 10 MIN | COOK TIME: 8 MIN | YIELD: 8 SERVINGS

INGREDIENTS

12 round baby potatoes

3 ounces cream cheese

4 slices cooked bacon, crumbled or chopped

2 green onions, finely chopped

½ cup grated cheddar cheese, divided

¼ cup sour cream

1 tablespoon milk

2 teaspoons hot sauce

DIRECTIONS

1 Preheat the air fryer to 320 degrees.

2 Poke holes into the baby potatoes with a fork. Place the potatoes onto a microwave-safe plate and microwave on high for 4 to 5 minutes, or until soft to squeeze. Let the potatoes cool until they're safe to handle, about 5 minutes.

3 Meanwhile, in a medium bowl, mix together the cream cheese, bacon, green onions, and ¼ cup of the cheddar cheese; set aside.

4 Slice the baby potatoes in half. Using a spoon, scoop out the pulp, leaving enough pulp on the inside to retain the shape of the potato half. Place the potato pulp into the cream cheese mixture and mash together with a fork. Using a spoon, refill the potato halves with filling.

5 Place the potato halves into the air fryer basket and top with the remaining ¼ cup of cheddar cheese.

6 Cook the loaded baked potato bites in batches for 8 minutes.

7 Meanwhile, make the sour cream sauce. In a small bowl, whisk together the sour cream, milk, and hot sauce. Add more hot sauce if desired.

8 When the potatoes have all finished cooking, place them onto a serving platter and serve with sour cream sauce drizzled over the top or as a dip.

NOTE: Microwave power varies. By gently squeezing the potato (while wearing oven mitts), you can see if the potato is cooked thoroughly. Adjust based on your microwave.

TIP: For a garnish, top with extra crumbled bacon and green onions.

Veggie Cheese Bites

PREP TIME: 10 MIN | **COOK TIME: 8 MIN** | **YIELD: 4 SERVINGS**

INGREDIENTS

2 cups riced vegetables (see the Note below)

½ cup shredded zucchini

½ teaspoon garlic powder

¼ teaspoon black pepper

¼ teaspoon salt

1 large egg

¾ cup shredded cheddar cheese

⅓ cup whole-wheat flour

DIRECTIONS

1 Preheat the air fryer to 350 degrees.

2 In a large bowl, mix together the riced vegetables, zucchini, garlic powder, pepper, and salt. Mix in the egg. Stir in the shredded cheese and whole-wheat flour until a thick, dough-like consistency forms. If you need to, add 1 teaspoon of flour at a time so you can mold the batter into balls.

3 Using a 1-inch scoop, portion the batter out into about 12 balls.

4 Liberally spray the air fryer basket with olive oil spray. Then place the veggie bites inside. Leave enough room between each bite so the air can flow around them.

5 Cook for 8 minutes, or until the outside is slightly browned. Depending on the size of your air fryer, you may need to cook these in batches.

6 Remove and let cool slightly before serving.

NOTE: We tested this recipe with a riced cauliflower and broccoli blend, but you can use whatever vegetables you have on hand.

VARY IT! Use your favorite herbs, spices, and cheese.

Spicy Sweet Potato Tater-Tots

PREP TIME: 1 HR 15 MIN	COOK TIME: 10 MIN	YIELD: 6 SERVINGS

INGREDIENTS

6 cups filtered water

2 medium sweet potatoes, peeled and cut in half

1 teaspoon garlic powder

½ teaspoon black pepper, divided

½ teaspoon salt, divided

1 cup panko breadcrumbs

1 teaspoon blackened seasoning

DIRECTIONS

1 In a large stovetop pot, bring the water to a boil. Add the sweet potatoes and let boil about 10 minutes, until a metal fork prong can be inserted but the potatoes still have a slight give (not completely mashed).

2 Carefully remove the potatoes from the pot and let cool.

3 When you're able to touch them, grate the potatoes into a large bowl. Mix the garlic powder, ¼ teaspoon of the black pepper, and ¼ teaspoon of the salt into the potatoes. Place the mixture in the refrigerator and let set at least 45 minutes (if you're leaving them longer than 45 minutes, cover the bowl).

4 Before assembling, mix the breadcrumbs and blackened seasoning in a small bowl.

5 Remove the sweet potatoes from the refrigerator and preheat the air fryer to 400 degrees.

6 Assemble the tater-tots by using a teaspoon to portion batter evenly and form into a tater-tot shape. Roll each tater-tot in the breadcrumb mixture. Then carefully place the tater-tots in the air fryer basket. Be sure that you've liberally sprayed the air fryer basket with an olive oil mist. Repeat until tater-tots fill the basket without touching one another. You'll need to do multiple batches, depending on the size of your air fryer.

7 Cook the tater-tots for 3 to 6 minutes, flip, and cook another 3 to 6 minutes.

8 Remove from the air fryer carefully and keep warm until ready to serve.

NOTE: Air fryer temperatures vary. Keep an eye on the tater-tots and flip them when the breading is browned.

TIP: To reheat leftover tater-tots, use the air fryer and cook at 350 degrees until ready to serve.

VARY IT! Prefer a cinnamon sugar tater-tot? Nix the garlic, pepper, and Cajun seasoning and use ½ teaspoon cinnamon and 2 teaspoons of sugar in the tater-tot, with 1 teaspoon of cinnamon and 2 tablespoons of cane sugar in the panko breading.

Homemade Pretzel Bites

PREP TIME: 1 HR 5 MIN	COOK TIME: 6 MIN	YIELD: 8 SERVINGS

INGREDIENTS

4¾ cups filtered water, divided

1 tablespoon butter

1 package fast-rising yeast

½ teaspoon salt

2⅓ cups bread flour

2 tablespoons baking soda

2 egg whites

1 teaspoon kosher salt

DIRECTIONS

1 Preheat the air fryer to 370 degrees.

2 In a large microwave-safe bowl, add ¾ cup of the water. Heat for 40 seconds in the microwave. Remove and whisk in the butter; then mix in the yeast and salt. Let sit 5 minutes.

3 Using a stand mixer with a dough hook attachment, add the yeast liquid and mix in the bread flour ⅓ cup at a time until all the flour is added and a dough is formed.

4 Remove the bowl from the stand; then let the dough rise 1 hour in a warm space, covered with a kitchen towel.

5 After the dough has doubled in size, remove from the bowl and punch down a few times on a lightly floured flat surface.

6 Divide the dough into 4 balls; then roll each ball out into a long, skinny, sticklike shape. Using a sharp knife, cut each dough stick into 6 pieces.

7 Repeat Step 6 for the remaining dough balls until you have about 24 bites formed.

8 Heat the remaining 4 cups of water over the stovetop in a medium pot with the baking soda stirred in.

9 Drop the pretzel bite dough into the hot water and let boil for 60 seconds, remove, and let slightly cool.

10 Lightly brush the top of each bite with the egg whites, and then cover with a pinch of kosher salt.

11 Spray the air fryer basket with olive oil spray and place the pretzel bites on top. Cook for 6 to 8 minutes, or until lightly browned. Remove and keep warm.

12 Repeat until all pretzel bites are cooked.

13 Serve warm.

Parmesan Pizza Nuggets

PREP TIME: 1 HR 5 MIN	COOK TIME: 6 MIN	YIELD: 8 SERVINGS

INGREDIENTS

¾ cup warm filtered water

1 package fast-rising yeast

½ teaspoon salt

2 cups all-purpose flour

¼ cup finely grated Parmesan cheese

1 teaspoon Italian seasoning

2 tablespoon extra-virgin olive oil

1 teaspoon kosher salt

DIRECTIONS

1 Preheat the air fryer to 370 degrees.

2 In a large microwave-safe bowl, add the water. Heat for 40 seconds in the microwave. Remove and mix in the yeast and salt. Let sit 5 minutes.

3 Meanwhile, in a medium bowl, mix the flour with the Parmesan cheese and Italian seasoning. Set aside.

4 Using a stand mixer with a dough hook attachment, add the yeast liquid and then mix in the flour mixture 1/3 cup at a time until all the flour mixture is added and a dough is formed.

5 Remove the bowl from the stand, and then let the dough rise for 1 hour in a warm space, covered with a kitchen towel.

6 After the dough has doubled in size, remove it from the bowl and punch it down a few times on a lightly floured flat surface.

7 Divide the dough into 4 balls, and then roll each ball out into a long, skinny, sticklike shape.

8 Using a sharp knife, cut each dough stick into 6 pieces. Repeat for the remaining dough balls until you have about 24 nuggets formed.

9 Lightly brush the top of each bite with the egg whites and cover with a pinch of sea salt.

10 Spray the air fryer basket with olive oil spray and place the pizza nuggets on top. Cook for 6 minutes, or until lightly browned. Remove and keep warm.

11 Repeat until all the nuggets are cooked.

12 Serve warm.

Cheesy Tortellini Bites

PREP TIME: 10 MIN	COOK TIME: 10 MIN	YIELD: 8 SERVINGS

INGREDIENTS

1 large egg

½ teaspoon black pepper

½ teaspoon garlic powder

1 teaspoon Italian seasoning

12 ounces frozen cheese tortellini

½ cup panko breadcrumbs

DIRECTIONS

1 Preheat the air fryer to 380 degrees.

2 Spray the air fryer basket with an olive-oil-based spray.

3 In a medium bowl, whisk the egg with the pepper, garlic powder, and Italian seasoning.

4 Dip the tortellini in the egg batter and then coat with the breadcrumbs. Place each tortellini in the basket, trying not to overlap them. You may need to cook in batches to ensure the even crisp all around.

5 Bake for 5 minutes, shake the basket, and bake another 5 minutes.

6 Remove and let cool 5 minutes. Serve with marinara sauce, ranch, or your favorite dressing.

NOTE: You can use leftover tortellini from a prior night's dinner that has already been cooked.

TIP: You can make these gluten-free by using a gluten-free tortellini and gluten-free breadcrumbs.

VARY IT! Prefer ravioli? Increase the cook time 5 to 7 minutes to ensure they're cooked thoroughly.

Bacon-Wrapped Goat Cheese Poppers

PREP TIME: 10 MIN	COOK TIME: 10 MIN	YIELD: 10 SERVINGS

INGREDIENTS

10 large jalapeño peppers

8 ounces goat cheese

10 slices bacon

DIRECTIONS

1 Preheat the air fryer to 380 degrees.

2 Slice the jalapeños in half. Carefully remove the veins and seeds of the jalapeños with a spoon.

3 Fill each jalapeño half with 2 teaspoons goat cheese.

4 Cut the bacon in half lengthwise to make long strips. Wrap the jalapeños with bacon, trying to cover the entire length of the jalapeño.

5 Place the bacon-wrapped jalapeños into the air fryer basket. Cook the stuffed jalapeños for 10 minutes or until bacon is crispy.

NOTE: If your skin is sensitive, use gloves when cutting and deseeding jalapeños to avoid irritation.

TIP: You can use cream cheese instead of goat cheese, if you prefer, but the sharp, sour notes of goat cheese add a fantastic balance of flavor to the spiciness of jalapeño and bacon.

Prosciutto Mozzarella Bites

PREP TIME: 10 MIN | **COOK TIME: 6 MIN** | **YIELD: 8 SERVINGS**

INGREDIENTS

8 pieces full-fat mozzarella string cheese

8 thin slices prosciutto

16 basil leaves

DIRECTIONS

1 Preheat the air fryer to 360 degrees.

2 Cut the string cheese in half across the center, not lengthwise. Do the same with the prosciutto.

3 Place a piece of prosciutto onto a clean workspace. Top the prosciutto with a basil leaf and then a piece of string cheese. Roll up the string cheese inside the prosciutto and secure with a wooden toothpick. Repeat with the remaining cheese sticks.

4 Place the prosciutto mozzarella bites into the air fryer basket and cook for 6 minutes, checking for doneness at 4 minutes.

NOTE: Do not use plastic toothpicks — they'll melt and be unsafe inside an air fryer.

TIP: A low-fat or fat-free cheese stick will not yield the same results.

Savory Sausage Balls

PREP TIME: 15 MIN | COOK TIME: 8 MIN | YIELD: 10 SERVINGS

INGREDIENTS

2 cups all-purpose flour

1 tablespoon baking powder

½ teaspoon garlic powder

¼ teaspoon onion powder

½ teaspoon salt

3 tablespoons milk

2½ cups grated pepper jack cheese

1 pound fresh sausage, casing removed

DIRECTIONS

1 Preheat the air fryer to 370 degrees.

2 In a large bowl, whisk together the flour, baking powder, garlic powder, onion powder, and salt. Add in the milk, grated cheese, and sausage.

3 Using a tablespoon, scoop out the sausage and roll it between your hands to form a rounded ball. You should end up with approximately 32 balls. Place them in the air fryer basket in a single layer and working in batches as necessary.

4 Cook for 8 minutes, or until the outer coating turns light brown.

5 Carefully remove, repeating with the remaining sausage balls.

NOTE: Breakfast sausage or Italian link sausages work well in this recipe.

Classic Chicken Wings

| PREP TIME: 5 MIN | COOK TIME: 20 MIN | YIELD: 8 SERVINGS |

INGREDIENTS

16 chicken wings

¼ cup all-purpose flour

¼ teaspoon garlic powder

¼ teaspoon paprika

½ teaspoon salt

½ teaspoon black pepper

¼ cup butter

½ cup hot sauce

½ teaspoon Worcestershire sauce

2 ounces crumbled blue cheese, for garnish

DIRECTIONS

1 Preheat the air fryer to 380 degrees.

2 Pat the chicken wings dry with paper towels.

3 In a medium bowl, mix together the flour, garlic powder, paprika, salt, and pepper. Toss the chicken wings with the flour mixture, dusting off any excess.

4 Place the chicken wings in the air fryer basket, making sure that the chicken wings aren't touching. Cook the chicken wings for 10 minutes, turn over, and cook another 5 minutes. Raise the temperature to 400 degrees and continue crisping the chicken wings for an additional 3 to 5 minutes.

5 Meanwhile, in a microwave-safe bowl, melt the butter and hot sauce for 1 to 2 minutes in the microwave. Remove from the microwave and stir in the Worcestershire sauce.

6 When the chicken wings have cooked, immediately transfer the chicken wings into the hot sauce mixture. Serve the coated chicken wings on a plate, and top with crumbled blue cheese.

NOTE: Two to three batches may be needed depending on the size of your air fryer. The more crowded your air fryer, the longer it will take for the chicken wings to get crispy.

NOTE: If your chicken wings are very meaty, increase the initial cook time to 20 minutes, and then raise the temperature and continue cooking for 3 to 5 minutes.

VARY IT! If spicy is not your thing, use barbecue sauce instead of hot sauce.

Chapter 8

Star-Studded Handhelds

I f you're a busy person at the beck and call of someone else's schedule (we're looking at you, multitasker moms), then this chapter is for you.

We're both fans of PB&J, but sometimes we like to treat ourselves with a gourmet handheld sandwich or wrap that makes us feel like we're dining out (when in reality, we're just trying to get something in our bellies between work and the next soccer practice!).

Whether you're a vegetarian or a carnivore, we promise there's a star-studded handheld in this chapter that will satisfy and satiate you! Now, who's ready to dive in?

Apple and Cheddar Grilled Cheese

PREP TIME: 10 MIN	COOK TIME: 7 MIN	YIELD: 1 SERVING

INGREDIENTS

2 slices seeded whole-grain bread

1 teaspoon extra-virgin olive oil

3 ounces cheddar cheese slices

½ small Honeycrisp apple, cored and thinly sliced

⅛ teaspoon black pepper

Salt, to taste

DIRECTIONS

1 Preheat the air fryer to 390 degrees.

2 Lay the bread down on a flat surface and lightly brush the outer sides with olive oil. Flip the slices of bread over and begin to assemble the sandwich.

3 Place 1½ ounces of cheese on the bread; then cover evenly with apple slices and top with a pinch of black pepper.

4 Top the apples with the remaining 1½ ounces of cheddar cheese; then cover with the other bread slice.

5 Spray the air fryer basket with an olive oil mist; then place the sandwich into the basket. Cook for 5 to 7 minutes, or until the cheese is melted and the outer edges of the bread are lightly browned.

NOTE: Depending on your air fryer basket and how it distributes heat, you may need to flip the sandwich halfway through cooking. Keep a close eye on it so it doesn't burn!

TIP: Use sliced cheese instead of shredded to prevent a cheesy mess in your air fryer.

VARY IT! Prefer a sandwich with a little heat? Use roasted red pepper and Pepper Jack cheese in place of apples and cheddar.

Fried Green Tomato BLT

INGREDIENTS

1 large green tomato

¼ teaspoon salt

¼ teaspoon pepper

½ cup panko breadcrumbs

¼ cup all-purpose flour

1 egg, whisked

4 slices bacon

4 slices sourdough bread

2 leaves lettuce

1 tablespoon mayonnaise

DIRECTIONS

1 Preheat the air fryer to 350 degrees for 3 minutes.

2 Slice the tomato into 4 thick slices. In a shallow bowl, mix together the salt, pepper, breadcrumbs, and flour.

3 Dip the tomato slices into the whisked egg and then into the flour mixture to create a breading. Spray liberally with cooking spray.

4 Place the breaded tomato slices into the air fryer basket on one side, and lay out the bacon in a single layer, slightly overlapping the bacon on the other side.

5 Cook for 5 minutes, flip over, and cook another 5 minutes, until desired crispness is achieved.

6 Meanwhile, toast the bread in a toaster.

7 To assemble sandwiches, place 1 leaf of lettuce on 2 slices of bread. On the other 2 slices, spread 1½ teaspoons mayonnaise on each slice. Place 2 slices of crisped bacon on top of the mayonnaise, and then place the tomatoes on top. Close the sandwiches, cut in half, and serve.

TIP: If you can't get your hands on green tomatoes, you can use traditional ripe tomatoes instead. Just slice and skip the breading.

Pesto Turkey Panini

PREP TIME: 5 MIN	COOK TIME: 5 MIN	YIELD: 1 SERVING

INGREDIENTS

2 slices whole-grain seeded bread

2 tablespoons pesto sauce

2 ounces deli turkey

2 slices Havarti cheese

1 slice tomato

DIRECTIONS

1 Preheat the air fryer to 350 degrees.

2 Lay the bread on a flat surface; then spread the pesto evenly on each slice of bread.

3 Place one slice of cheese on top of each bread slice; then put 2 ounces of deli turkey on top.

4 Place the tomato slice on top of the turkey; then cover with the remaining slice of cheese and bread.

5 Liberally spray the outside of the bread with an olive oil mist; then place inside the air fryer basket.

6 Cook for 3 minutes, flip, and cook another 3 minutes, or until the cheese melts and the outside of the bread is toasted. Remove from the air fryer and serve warm with desired sides.

NOTE: Want to double the recipe? No problem! Just double the portion of each ingredient.

TIP: Make your own homemade pesto! See Chapter 17.

VARY IT! Prefer a different deli meat or cheese? Swap them in for the turkey and Havarti.

Mediterranean Roasted Vegetable Panini

PREP TIME: 10 MIN	COOK TIME: 13 MIN	YIELD: 2 SERVINGS

INGREDIENTS

½ red bell pepper, sliced into long strips

4 small mushrooms

1 small zucchini, sliced into 4 lengthwise strips

2 tablespoons extra-virgin olive oil

1 teaspoon dried oregano

½ teaspoon sea salt

4 slices sourdough bread or French bread

2 ounces mozzarella cheese, sliced

DIRECTIONS

1 Preheat the air fryer to 400 degrees.

2 In a medium bowl, place the bell pepper, mushrooms, and zucchini. Toss with the olive oil, oregano, and sea salt. Using tongs, place the vegetables into the air fryer basket. Roast the vegetables for 6 minutes.

3 Meanwhile, brush the sides of the bread with the remaining seasoned olive oil. As you assemble the sandwiches, the olive-oil-coated slices will become the outside of the sandwiches.

4 Remove the vegetables from the air fryer. Slice the roasted mushrooms. Place the roasted vegetables onto twice slices of bread and top each sandwich with 1 ounce sliced mozzarella cheese. Top with the remaining bread slices.

5 Reduce the temperature to 390 degrees. Place the sandwiches back into the air fryer basket. Cook for 5 to 7 minutes or until golden brown and the cheese is melted.

NOTE: Depending on your air fryer basket and how it distributes heat, you may need to flip the sandwiches halfway through cooking. Keep a close eye on them so they don't burn!

VARY IT! Prefer Mexican flavors? Add ground cumin to the olive oil mixture and use Pepper Jack cheese instead of mozzarella.

Tuna Melt

| PREP TIME: 15 MIN | COOK TIME: 8 MIN | YIELD: 2 SERVINGS |

INGREDIENTS

5 ounces canned tuna in water, no salt added

2 tablespoons finely chopped onion

1 tablespoon mayonnaise

1 tablespoon plain Greek yogurt

⅛ teaspoon dill

¼ teaspoon ground black pepper

⅛ teaspoon salt

4 slices whole-grain bread

1 teaspoon extra-virgin olive oil

4 slices white cheddar cheese, divided

8 dill pickle slices

DIRECTIONS

1 Preheat the air fryer to 390 degrees.

2 In a medium bowl, mix the tuna, onion, mayonnaise, yogurt, dill, pepper, and salt. Set aside.

3 Lay the bread flat; then lightly brush the outer sides with the olive oil.

4 Flip the bread over, and place 1 slice of cheese down on 2 slices of bread. Spread half of the tuna mixture on each of those 2 slices of bread; then place 4 dill pickle circles on top of each. Add the remaining slice of cheese and cover with the bread (oiled side facing out).

5 Place each sandwich inside the air fryer basket. Cook for 4 minutes, rotate, and cook another 4 minutes to evenly melt the cheese and crisp the bread.

6 Remove from the air fryer and let cool 3 minutes before slicing. Serve warm.

TIP: Prepare the tuna ahead of time and assemble the sandwiches when you're ready. Tuna will keep in the refrigerator for 3 days in an airtight container.

TIP: Serve with a side salad or preferred chip from Chapter 10.

Turkey Reuben

PREP TIME: 10 MIN | COOK TIME: 8 MIN | YIELD: 2 SERVINGS

INGREDIENTS

1 teaspoon extra-virgin olive oil

4 slices rye bread

2 tablespoons Russian dressing

6 ounces turkey pastrami

4 ounces sauerkraut

2 slices Swiss cheese

DIRECTIONS

1 Preheat the air fryer to 390 degrees.

2 Place the bread down on a flat surface, and lightly brush the outer edges with oil.

3 On 2 slices of the bread, spread 1 tablespoon of Russian dressing on the opposite side of the oil.

4 On the 2 slices with dressing, place half of the turkey pastrami on top of the dressing, followed by half of the sauerkraut.

5 Top each sandwich with 1 slice of Swiss cheese; then place the remaining slice of bread over the top. Cook for 4 minutes per side, carefully flip, and cook another 4 minutes.

6 Remove from the air fryer and let cool 3 to 5 minutes. Slice in half and serve warm.

TIP: Enjoy immediately. These sandwiches don't reheat well.

Build Your Own Hot Pocket

PREP TIME: 10 MIN	COOK TIME: 7 MIN	YIELD: 6 SERVINGS

INGREDIENTS

1 pound store-bought or homemade whole-wheat pizza dough

1½ cups diced ham or cooked turkey

1½ cups grated cheddar cheese (or cheese of your choice)

DIRECTIONS

1 Preheat the air fryer to 370 degrees.

2 Place the dough on a floured surface. Using a rolling pin, roll out the dough into a large square, about ½ inch thick. Using a pizza cutter or dough scraper, cut the dough into twelve 2½-x-4-inch rectangles.

3 Place 2 tablespoons chopped ham or turkey and 2 tablespoons grated cheese down the center of 6 of the dough rectangles. Place the other six rectangles on top. To sandwich the top and bottom pieces together, use the tines of the fork to press together the edges. Poke the surface of the top piece with the fork to create a vent to release steam while cooking.

4 Spray the surface of the hot pocket with cooking spray. Place 3 or 4 hot pockets into air fryer basket and cook for 5 to 7 minutes or until golden brown. Remove from the air fryer and let rest for 2 minutes before serving.

TIP: You can make small hot pockets for young children or appetizers by cutting the dough into 2-x-3-inch rectangles.

VARY IT! If you prefer a vegetarian option, opt for broccoli instead of ham or turkey. Use blanched broccoli that has been patted dry and chopped.

Calzones

PREP TIME: 10 MIN	COOK TIME: 10 MIN	YIELD: 4 SERVINGS

INGREDIENTS

1 pound store-bought or homemade whole-wheat pizza dough

1½ cups jarred marinara sauce, divided

2 cups fresh baby spinach leaves

1⅓ cups shredded mozzarella cheese

¼ cup chopped red onions

¼ cup chopped red bell peppers

1 cup cooked Italian sausage, drained and rinsed

DIRECTIONS

1 Preheat the air fryer to 360 degrees.

2 Divide the dough into 4 equal pieces. On a lightly floured surface, roll out one piece into an 8-inch circle. Spread 2 tablespoons of marinara sauce onto the dough. Next, top half of the dough with ½ cup spinach leaves, ⅓ cup mozzarella, 1 tablespoon onions, 1 tablespoon bell peppers, and ¼ cup sausage. Fold the other half of dough over the top and, using a fork, crimp the edges to seal. Poke the surface of the top piece with the fork to create a vent to release steam while cooking. Repeat until four calzones are prepared.

3 Place 2 calzones into the air fryer basket. Bake for 10 to 12 minutes or until golden brown and cooked through.

NOTE: The best way to know if your calzone is cooked completely is to use a food thermometer and cook until 160 degrees internal temperature is reached.

VARY IT! Much like a pizza, you can create any flavor combination of calzones.

Tex Mex Quesadilla

PREP TIME: 14 MIN	COOK TIME: 8 MIN	YIELD: 2 SERVINGS

INGREDIENTS

¼ pound lean ground beef

½ teaspoon minced garlic

¼ cup chopped onion

½ teaspoon taco seasoning

1 teaspoon extra-virgin olive oil

Two 8-inch flour tortillas

¼ cup cooked pinto beans, mashed

½ cup shredded Mexican cheese

1 tablespoon barbecue sauce

2 tablespoon chopped cilantro

DIRECTIONS

1 In a skillet over medium-high heat on the stovetop, brown the beef. Stir in the garlic, onion, and taco seasoning, and let the ingredients cook together. When the beef is cooked, remove from the stovetop and let cool.

2 Preheat the air fryer to 370 degrees.

3 Place the flour tortillas on a flat surface and spread 2 tablespoons of mashed beans on each tortilla. Top one tortilla with ¼ cup shredded cheese and then half of the ground beef mixture.

4 Sprinkle the remaining shredded cheese on top. Cover with the other tortilla, bean side down.

5 Spray the air fryer basket with an olive oil spray and carefully place the quesadilla into it.

6 Cook for 7 to 9 minutes, or until the cheese melts and the outer tortilla edges are lightly crisped and browned.

7 Remove from the basket and let cool 5 minutes. Drizzle barbecue sauce over the top, and sprinkle with cilantro. Slice into quarters and serve warm.

NOTE Use large spatulas to help transfer the quesadilla.

TIP: Prefer a little spice? Add 1 seeded and diced jalapeño pepper into the beef.

VARY IT! Prefer chicken in place of beef? No meat? The possibilities are endless to make this quesadilla your own.

Buffalo Chicken Wrap

PREP TIME: 10 MIN	COOK TIME: 8 MIN	YIELD: 4 SERVINGS

INGREDIENTS

8 ounce chicken breasts, cubed

½ teaspoon salt

¼ teaspoon black pepper

1 tablespoon butter

1 tablespoon vegetable oil

¼ cup hot sauce

Four 8-inch flour tortillas

1 cup shredded cabbage or lettuce

1 rib celery, cut into julienned strips (matchsticks)

¼ cup crumbled blue cheese

DIRECTIONS

1 Preheat the air fryer to 400 degrees.

2 Pat the chicken breasts dry with a paper towel. Season the cubed chicken breasts with salt and pepper. Cook the chicken breasts for 6 to 8 minutes or until completely cooked.

3 Meanwhile, in a microwave-safe bowl, combine the butter, vegetable oil, and hot sauce in the microwave for 30 seconds, stir, and heat for an additional 30 seconds or until the butter has melted.

4 After the chicken has cooked, add the chicken into the hot sauce mixture and toss to coat the chicken pieces.

5 To assemble the wraps, place 4 tortillas onto 4 plates. Place ¼ cup shredded cabbage or lettuce onto each tortilla. Top the cabbage equally with buffalo chicken; then top with celery sticks and crumbled blue cheese. Fold up the sides and serve.

NOTE: Test a large piece of chicken to ensure all pieces have fully cooked. If you see any pink, continue cooking for 1 to 2 minutes and use a clean utensil to recheck the chicken.

Chapter 9

Savory Sides

This chapter helps you explore the possibilities of the air fryer! From air frying your Street Corn to making the perfect batch of Cajun Curly Fries, you'll soon find out you won't be sacrificing any flavor by taking away the deep-fried fat.

Plus, the air fryer is the perfect way to roast your favorite vegetables. Our Roasted Brussels Sprouts, Fried Okra, and Bacon-Wrapped Asparagus are just a few that have easily become family favorites in just a short time. Use this chapter as a guide, and let your creativity flow to allow your own favorite vegetables to become the star of your side dishes with the air fryer.

Asiago Broccoli

PREP TIME: 10 MIN	COOK TIME: 14 MIN	YIELD: 4 SERVINGS

INGREDIENTS

1 head broccoli, cut into florets

1 tablespoon extra-virgin olive oil

1 teaspoon minced garlic

¼ teaspoon ground black pepper

¼ teaspoon salt

¼ cup asiago cheese

DIRECTIONS

1 Preheat the air fryer to 360 degrees.

2 In a medium bowl, toss the broccoli florets with the olive oil, garlic, pepper, and salt. Lightly spray the air fryer basket with olive oil spray.

3 Place the broccoli florets into the basket and cook for 7 minutes. Shake the basket and sprinkle the broccoli with cheese. Cook another 7 minutes.

4 Remove from the basket and serve warm.

Moroccan Cauliflower

PREP TIME: 10 MIN | COOK TIME: 15 MIN | YIELD: 6 SERVINGS

INGREDIENTS

1 tablespoon curry powder

2 teaspoons smoky paprika

½ teaspoon ground cumin

½ teaspoon salt

1 head cauliflower, cut into bite-size pieces

¼ cup red wine vinegar

2 tablespoons extra-virgin olive oil

2 tablespoons chopped parsley

DIRECTIONS

1 Preheat the air fryer to 370 degrees.

2 In a large bowl, mix the curry powder, paprika, cumin, and salt. Add the cauliflower and stir to coat. Pour the red wine vinegar over the top and continue stirring.

3 Place the cauliflower into the air fryer basket; drizzle olive oil over the top.

4 Cook the cauliflower for 5 minutes, toss, and cook another 5 minutes. Raise the temperature to 400 degrees and continue cooking for 4 to 6 minutes, or until crispy.

Roasted Brussels Sprouts

PREP TIME: 10 MIN	COOK TIME: 25 MIN	YIELD: 4 SERVINGS

INGREDIENTS

½ cup balsamic vinegar

2 tablespoons honey

1 pound Brussels sprouts, halved lengthwise

2 slices bacon, chopped

½ teaspoon garlic powder

1 teaspoon salt

1 tablespoon extra-virgin olive oil

¼ cup grated Parmesan cheese

DIRECTIONS

1 Preheat the air fryer to 370 degrees.

2 In a small saucepan, heat the vinegar and honey for 8 to 10 minutes over medium-low heat, or until the balsamic vinegar reduces by half to create a thick balsamic glazing sauce.

3 While the balsamic glaze is reducing, in a large bowl, toss together the Brussels sprouts, bacon, garlic powder, salt, and olive oil. Pour the mixture into the air fryer basket and cook for 10 minutes; check for doneness. Cook another 2 to 5 minutes or until slightly crispy and tender.

4 Pour the balsamic glaze into a serving bowl and add the cooked Brussels sprouts to the dish, stirring to coat. Top with grated Parmesan cheese and serve.

Fried Okra

INGREDIENTS

1 pound okra

1 large egg

1 tablespoon milk

1 teaspoon salt, divided

½ teaspoon black pepper, divided

¼ teaspoon paprika

¼ teaspoon thyme

½ cup cornmeal

½ cup all-purpose flour

DIRECTIONS

1 Preheat the air fryer to 400 degrees.

2 Cut the okra into ½-inch rounds.

3 In a medium bowl, whisk together the egg, milk, ½ teaspoon of the salt, and ¼ teaspoon of black pepper. Place the okra into the egg mixture and toss until well coated.

4 In a separate bowl, mix together the remaining ½ teaspoon of salt, the remaining ¼ teaspoon of black pepper, the paprika, the thyme, the cornmeal, and the flour. Working in small batches, dredge the egg-coated okra in the cornmeal mixture until all the okra has been breaded.

5 Place a single layer of okra in the air fryer basket and spray with cooking spray. Cook for 4 minutes, toss to check for crispness, and cook another 4 minutes. Repeat in batches, as needed.

NOTE: If you're using frozen okra, defrost and pat dry prior to using.

TIP: Serve with ranch dip.

Street Corn

INGREDIENTS

1 tablespoon butter

4 ears corn

⅓ cup plain Greek yogurt

2 tablespoons Parmesan cheese

½ teaspoon paprika

½ teaspoon garlic powder

¼ teaspoon salt

¼ teaspoon black pepper

¼ cup finely chopped cilantro

DIRECTIONS

1 Preheat the air fryer to 400 degrees.

2 In a medium microwave-safe bowl, melt the butter in the microwave. Lightly brush the outside of the ears of corn with the melted butter.

3 Place the corn into the air fryer basket and cook for 5 minutes, flip the corn, and cook another 5 minutes.

4 Meanwhile, in a medium bowl, mix the yogurt, cheese, paprika, garlic powder, salt, and pepper. Set aside.

5 Carefully remove the corn from the air fryer and let cool 3 minutes. Brush the outside edges with the yogurt mixture and top with fresh chopped cilantro. Serve immediately.

NOTE: Cooking for fewer people? Cut the recipe in half.

TIP: You can reheat the corn in the air fryer without sauce for 1 to 2 minutes at 370 degrees.

VARY IT! You can use another variety of cheese if Parmesan isn't your favorite or you have something else on hand.

Panko-Crusted Zucchini Fries

PREP TIME: 15 MIN	COOK TIME: 8 MIN	YIELD: 6 SERVINGS

INGREDIENTS

3 medium zucchinis

½ cup flour

1 teaspoon salt, divided

½ teaspoon black pepper, divided

¾ teaspoon dried thyme, divided

2 large eggs

1 ½ cups whole-wheat or plain panko breadcrumbs

½ cup grated Parmesan cheese

DIRECTIONS

1 Preheat the air fryer to 380 degrees.

2 Slice the zucchinis in half lengthwise, then into long strips about ½-inch thick, like thick fries.

3 In a medium bowl, mix the flour, ½ teaspoon of the salt, ¼ teaspoon of the black pepper, and ½ teaspoon of thyme.

4 In a separate bowl, whisk together the eggs, ½ teaspoon of the salt, and ¼ teaspoon of the black pepper.

5 In a third bowl, combine the breadcrumbs, cheese, and the remaining ¼ teaspoon of dried thyme.

6 Working with one zucchini fry at a time, dip the zucchini fry first into the flour mixture, then into the whisked eggs, and finally into the breading. Repeat until all the fries are breaded.

7 Place the zucchini fries into the air fryer basket, spray with cooking spray, and cook for 4 minutes; shake the basket and cook another 4 to 6 minutes or until golden brown and crispy.

8 Remove and serve warm.

TIP: Serve with lemon and garlic yogurt dipping sauce or ranch dressing.

VARY IT! You can use yellow summer squash in this recipe if you want.

Parmesan Garlic Fries

PREP TIME: 10 MIN	COOK TIME: 20 MIN	YIELD: 4 SERVINGS

INGREDIENTS

2 medium Yukon gold potatoes, washed

1 tablespoon extra-virgin olive oil

1 garlic clove, minced

2 tablespoons finely grated parmesan cheese

¼ teaspoon black pepper

¼ teaspoon salt

1 tablespoon freshly chopped parsley

DIRECTIONS

1 Preheat the air fryer to 400 degrees.

2 Slice the potatoes into long strips about ¼-inch thick. In a large bowl, toss the potatoes with the olive oil, garlic, cheese, pepper, and salt.

3 Place the fries into the air fryer basket and cook for 4 minutes; shake the basket and cook another 4 minutes.

4 Remove and serve warm.

NOTE: Do not stack the fries! You may need to make them in two batches to evenly cook and get that crisp texture.

TIP: You can make these potatoes into wedges, too. Adjust the cooking time by 2 to 3 minutes depending on the thickness of your potatoes.

VARY IT! You can use truffle oil in place of olive oil or your spices if you prefer.

Sweet Potato Curly Fries

PREP TIME: 15 MIN | COOK TIME: 10 MIN | YIELD: 4 SERVINGS

INGREDIENTS

2 medium sweet potatoes, washed

2 tablespoons avocado oil

¾ teaspoon salt, divided

1 medium avocado

½ teaspoon garlic powder

½ teaspoon paprika

¼ teaspoon black pepper

½ juice lime

3 tablespoons fresh cilantro

DIRECTIONS

1 Preheat the air fryer to 400 degrees.

2 Using a spiralizer, create curly spirals with the sweet potatoes. Keep the pieces about 1½ inches long. Continue until all the potatoes are used.

3 In a large bowl, toss the curly sweet potatoes with the avocado oil and ½ teaspoon of the salt.

4 Place the potatoes in the air fryer basket and cook for 5 minutes; shake and cook another 5 minutes.

5 While cooking, add the avocado, garlic, paprika, pepper, the remaining ¼ teaspoon of salt, lime juice, and cilantro to a blender and process until smooth. Set aside.

6 When cooking completes, remove the fries and serve warm with the lime avocado sauce.

NOTE: Depending on the size of your air fryer, you may need to cook the fries in batches for an even crisp.

TIP: Tight on time? You can buy prepared spiralized sweet potato zoodles in the produce section of your market. Cut into 1½ inch pieces.

VARY IT! Prefer a spicy or sweet fry? Toss fries with 1 teaspoon of Cajun seasoning for a kick or mix ½ teaspoon ground cinnamon with 1 teaspoon cane sugar for something sweeter.

Crispy Herbed Potatoes

PREP TIME: 5 MIN | COOK TIME: 20 MIN | YIELD: 6 SERVINGS

INGREDIENTS

3 medium baking potatoes, washed and cubed

½ teaspoon dried thyme

1 teaspoon minced dried rosemary

½ teaspoon garlic powder

1 teaspoon sea salt

½ teaspoon black pepper

2 tablespoons extra-virgin olive oil

¼ cup chopped parsley

DIRECTIONS

1 Preheat the air fryer to 390 degrees.

2 Pat the potatoes dry. In a large bowl, mix together the cubed potatoes, thyme, rosemary, garlic powder, sea salt, and pepper. Drizzle and toss with olive oil.

3 Pour the herbed potatoes into the air fryer basket. Cook for 20 minutes, stirring every 5 minutes.

4 Toss the cooked potatoes with chopped parsley and serve immediately.

VARY IT! Potatoes are versatile — add any spice or seasoning mixture you prefer and create your own favorite side dish.

Breakfast Chimichangas (Chapter 5)

Chocolate Chip Banana Muffins (Chapter 6)

Avocado Fries (Chapter 7)

Homemade Pretzel Bites (Chapter 7)

Tuna Melt (Chapter 8)

Asiago Broccoli (Chapter 9)

Street Corn (Chapter 9)

Gluten-Free Nutty Chicken Fingers (Chapter 11)

Southwest Gluten-Free Turkey Meatloaf (Chapter 11)

Pork Schnitzel (Chapter 11)

Honey Pecan Shrimp (Chapter 12)

Charred Cauliflower Tacos (Chapter 13)

Spicy Sesame Tempeh Slaw with Peanut Dressing (Chapter 13)

Black Bean Empanadas (Chapter 13)

Honey-Roasted Mixed Nuts (Chapter 14)

Thumbprint Sugar Cookies (Chapter 14)

Mashed Potato Pancakes

PREP TIME: 10 MIN | COOK TIME: 10 MIN | YIELD: 6 SERVINGS

INGREDIENTS

2 cups leftover mashed potatoes

½ cup grated cheddar cheese

¼ cup thinly sliced green onions

½ teaspoon salt

¼ teaspoon black pepper

1 cup breadcrumbs

DIRECTIONS

1 Preheat the air fryer to 380 degrees.

2 In a large bowl, mix together the potatoes, cheese, and onions. Using a ¼ cup measuring cup, measure out 6 patties. Form the potatoes into ½-inch thick patties. Season the patties with salt and pepper on both sides.

3 In a small bowl, place the breadcrumbs. Gently press the potato pancakes into the breadcrumbs.

4 Place the potato pancakes into the air fryer basket and spray with cooking spray. Cook for 5 minutes, turn the pancakes over, and cook another 3 to 5 minutes or until golden brown on the outside and cooked through on the inside.

TIP: Serve with sour cream, sunny-side-up eggs, or applesauce.

VARY IT! Leftover mashed sweet potatoes work well in this dish, too! Just use Monterey Jack cheese instead of cheddar.

Bacon-Wrapped Asparagus

PREP TIME: 5 MIN | **COOK TIME: 10 MIN** | **YIELD: 4 SERVINGS**

INGREDIENTS

1 tablespoon extra-virgin olive oil

½ teaspoon sea salt

¼ cup grated Parmesan cheese

1 pound asparagus, ends trimmed

8 slices bacon

DIRECTIONS

1 Preheat the air fryer to 380 degrees.

2 In large bowl, mix together the olive oil, sea salt, and Parmesan cheese. Toss the asparagus in the olive oil mixture.

3 Evenly divide the asparagus into 8 bundles. Wrap 1 piece of bacon around each bundle, not overlapping the bacon but spreading it across the bundle.

4 Place the asparagus bundles into the air fryer basket, not touching. Work in batches as needed.

5 Cook for 8 minutes; check for doneness, and cook another 2 minutes.

NOTE: If you're working with thin, baby asparagus, check after 6 minutes.

Chicken Eggrolls

| PREP TIME: 25 MIN | COOK TIME: 17 MIN | YIELD: 10 SERVINGS |

INGREDIENTS

1 tablespoon vegetable oil

¼ cup chopped onion

1 clove garlic, minced

1 cup shredded carrot

½ cup thinly sliced celery

2 cups cooked chicken

2 cups shredded white cabbage

½ cup teriyaki sauce

20 egg roll wrappers

1 egg, whisked

1 tablespoon water

DIRECTIONS

1 Preheat the air fryer to 390 degrees.

2 In a large skillet, heat the oil over medium-high heat. Add in the onion and sauté for 1 minute. Add in the garlic and sauté for 30 seconds. Add in the carrot and celery and cook for 2 minutes. Add in the chicken, cabbage, and teriyaki sauce. Allow the mixture to cook for 1 minute, stirring to combine. Remove from the heat.

3 In a small bowl, whisk together the egg and water for brushing the edges.

4 Lay the eggroll wrappers out at an angle. Place ¼ cup filling in the center. Fold the bottom corner up first and then fold in the corners; roll up to complete eggroll.

5 Place the eggrolls in the air fryer basket, spray with cooking spray, and cook for 8 minutes, turn over, and cook another 2 to 4 minutes.

NOTE: You can use store-bought coleslaw mix in place of cabbage, carrots, and celery.

TIP: Rotisserie chicken makes this meal pull together in a snap!

TIP: Serve with sweet-and-sour sauce or spicy mustard.

VARY IT! Add a southwestern twist with fresh cilantro and corn.

Panzanella Salad with Crispy Croutons

PREP TIME: 10 MIN	COOK TIME: 3 MIN	YIELD: 4 SERVINGS

INGREDIENTS

½ French baguette, sliced in half lengthwise

2 large cloves garlic

2 large ripe tomatoes, divided

2 small Persian cucumbers, quartered and diced

¼ cup Kalamata olives

1 tablespoon chopped, fresh oregano or 1 teaspoon dried oregano

¼ cup chopped fresh basil

¼ cup chopped fresh parsley

½ cup sliced red onion

2 tablespoons red wine vinegar

¼ cup extra-virgin olive oil

Salt and pepper, to taste

DIRECTIONS

1 Preheat the air fryer to 380 degrees.

2 Place the baguette into the air fryer and toast for 3 to 5 minutes or until lightly golden brown.

3 Remove the bread from air fryer and immediately rub 1 raw garlic clove firmly onto the inside portion of each piece of bread, scraping the garlic onto the bread.

4 Slice 1 of the tomatoes in half and rub the cut edge of one half of the tomato onto the toasted bread. Season the rubbed bread with sea salt to taste.

5 Cut the bread into cubes and place in a large bowl. Cube the remaining 1½ tomatoes and add to the bowl. Add the cucumbers, olives, oregano, basil, parsley, and onion; stir to mix. Drizzle the red wine vinegar into the bowl, and stir. Drizzle the olive oil over the top, stir, and adjust the seasonings with salt and pepper.

6 Serve immediately or allow to sit at room temperature up to 1 hour before serving.

NOTE: This salad is best served the day you prepare it.

TIP: Use fresh herbs and summer-ripe vegetables when you can.

VARY IT! If you can't find olives, use 2 tablespoons capers instead.

Chapter **10**

Everything Chips

Whether you're craving something sweet or salty, this chapter shows you how to create the perfect snack using your air fryer. From savory beet chips to classic potato chips to sinfully sweet cinnamon apple or sweet potato chips, you'll walk away with something delicious to nosh on this week.

But don't just stop with the recipes in this chapter! Use these recipes for inspiration and let your creativity (and the produce you have on hand) be your guide as you explore the wonderful array of fruits and vegetables that can become a delicious and nutritious chip in mere minutes.

Beet Chips

PREP TIME: 40 MIN	COOK TIME: 20 MIN	YIELD: 4 SERVINGS

INGREDIENTS

2 large red beets, washed and skinned

1 tablespoon avocado oil

¼ teaspoon salt

DIRECTIONS

1 Preheat the air fryer to 330 degrees.

2 Using a mandolin or sharp knife, slice the beets in ⅛-inch slices. Place them in a bowl of water and let them soak for 30 minutes. Drain the water and pat the beets dry with a paper towel or kitchen cloth.

3 In a medium bowl, toss the beets with avocado oil and sprinkle them with salt.

4 Lightly spray the air fryer basket with olive oil mist and place the beet chips into the basket. To allow for even cooking, don't overlap the beets; cook in batches if necessary.

5 Cook the beet chips 15 to 20 minutes, shaking the basket every 5 minutes, until the outer edges of the beets begin to flip up like a chip. Remove from the basket and serve warm. Repeat with the remaining chips until they're all cooked.

NOTE: Depending on the size of your air fryer, you may need to cook in multiple batches.

NOTE: Be sure to use a kitchen towel you don't care about! Red beets bleed a lot and the purple color is hard to get out of fabric (including your clothes).

TIP: Monitor your air fryer temperature closely to prevent burning the beets. Some air fryers get hotter than others, so keep an eye on them.

Carrot Chips

PREP TIME: 10 MIN   COOK TIME: 10 MIN   YIELD: 4 SERVINGS

INGREDIENTS

1 pound carrots, thinly sliced

2 tablespoons extra-virgin olive oil

¼ teaspoon garlic powder

¼ teaspoon black pepper

½ teaspoon salt

DIRECTIONS

1   Preheat the air fryer to 390 degrees.

2   In a medium bowl, toss the carrot slices with the olive oil, garlic powder, pepper, and salt.

3   Liberally spray the air fryer basket with olive oil mist.

4   Place the carrot slices in the air fryer basket. To allow for even cooking, don't overlap the carrots; cook in batches if necessary.

5   Cook for 5 minutes, shake the basket, and cook another 5 minutes.

6   Remove from the basket and serve warm. Repeat with the remaining carrot slices until they're all cooked.

NOTE: Depending on the size of your air fryer, you may need to cook in multiple batches.

TIP: Purchase presliced carrot chips in the produce section of your local market to save time on prep.

Cinnamon Apple Crisps

PREP TIME: 3 MIN	COOK TIME: 22 MIN	YIELD: 1 SERVING

INGREDIENTS

1 large apple

½ teaspoon ground cinnamon

2 teaspoons avocado oil or coconut oil

DIRECTIONS

1 Preheat the air fryer to 300 degrees.

2 Using a mandolin or knife, slice the apples to ¼-inch thickness. Pat the apples dry with a paper towel or kitchen cloth. Sprinkle the apple slices with ground cinnamon. Spray or drizzle the oil over the top of the apple slices and toss to coat.

3 Place the apple slices in the air fryer basket. To allow for even cooking, don't overlap the slices; cook in batches if necessary.

4 Cook for 20 minutes, shaking the basket every 5 minutes. After 20 minutes, increase the air fryer temperature to 330 degrees and cook another 2 minutes, shaking the basket every 30 seconds. Remove the apples from the basket before they get too dark.

5 Spread the chips out onto paper towels to cool completely, at least 5 minutes. Repeat with the remaining apple slices until they're all cooked.

NOTE: Gala and Fuji apples are great for sweet apples and Granny Smith is tasty if you like tart apples.

TIP: If your chips are getting burned, try slicing them slightly thicker and decreasing the final cooking temperature to 320 degrees.

VARY IT! Cardamom, ginger, and nutmeg are fun alternatives to cinnamon.

Classic Potato Chips

PREP TIME: 40 MIN	COOK TIME: 8 MIN	YIELD: 4 SERVINGS

INGREDIENTS

2 medium russet potatoes, washed

2 cups filtered water

1 tablespoon avocado oil

½ teaspoon salt

DIRECTIONS

1 Using a mandolin, slice the potatoes into ⅛-inch-thick pieces.

2 Pour the water into a large bowl. Place the potatoes in the bowl and soak for at least 30 minutes.

3 Preheat the air fryer to 350 degrees.

4 Drain the water and pat the potatoes dry with a paper towel or kitchen cloth. Toss with avocado oil and salt. Liberally spray the air fryer basket with olive oil mist.

5 Set the potatoes inside the air fryer basket, separating them so they're not on top of each other. Cook for 5 minutes, shake the basket, and cook another 5 minutes, or until browned.

6 Remove and let cool a few minutes prior to serving. Repeat until all the chips are cooked.

NOTE: Chips are best served immediately. You can store them, but they tend to lose their crispness over a few hours. You can reheat them in the air fryer if you make a big batch, but they taste the best when first cooked!

VARY IT! Add 1 teaspoon of your favorite seasoning spice mix from Chapter 2 before you toss them in the air fryer.

Corn Tortilla Chips

PREP TIME: 5 MIN	COOK TIME: 12 MIN	YIELD: 4 SERVINGS

INGREDIENTS

Eight 6-inch corn tortillas

½ teaspoon sea salt

¼ teaspoon ground cumin

¼ teaspoon chili powder

¼ teaspoon garlic powder

⅛ teaspoon onion powder

1 tablespoon avocado oil

DIRECTIONS

1 Cut each corn tortilla into quarters, creating 32 chips in total.

2 Preheat the air fryer to 350 degrees.

3 In a small bowl, mix together the sea salt, cumin, chili powder, garlic powder, and onion powder.

4 Spray or brush one side of the tortillas with avocado oil. Sprinkle the seasoning mixture evenly over the oiled side of the chips.

5 Working in batches, place half the chips in the air fryer basket. Cook for 8 minutes, shake the basket, and cook another 2 to 4 minutes, checking for crispness. When the chips are golden brown, spread them out onto paper towels and allow them to cool for 3 minutes before serving. Repeat with the remaining chips.

NOTE: If the chips are getting too dark, reduce the temperature by 10 to 20 degrees.

TIP: Serve with your favorite guacamole or fresh pico de gallo.

VARY IT! If you prefer flour tortillas, you can use those instead of corn.

Garlic Parmesan Kale Chips

PREP TIME: 3 MIN	COOK TIME: 6 MIN	YIELD: 2 SERVINGS

INGREDIENTS

16 large kale leaves, washed and thick stems removed

1 tablespoon avocado oil

½ teaspoon garlic powder

1 teaspoon soy sauce or tamari

¼ cup grated Parmesan cheese

DIRECTIONS

1 Preheat the air fryer to 370 degrees.

2 Make a stack of kale leaves and cut them into 4 pieces.

3 Place the kale pieces into a large bowl. Drizzle the avocado oil onto the kale and rub to coat. Add the garlic powder, soy sauce or tamari, and cheese, tossing to coat.

4 Pour the chips into the air fryer basket and cook for 3 minutes, shake the basket, and cook another 3 minutes, checking for crispness every minute. When done cooking, pour the kale chips onto paper towels and cool at least 5 minutes before serving.

NOTE: Tuscan or lacinato kale is our favorite, but all kale and chard greens work well with this recipe.

VARY IT! For a vegan option try using coconut aminos instead of soy sauce, and skip the Parmesan cheese. Toss with nutritional yeast after the chips have been baked.

Parmesan Crackers

PREP TIME: 5 MIN	COOK TIME: 6 MIN	YIELD: 6 SERVINGS

INGREDIENTS

2 cups finely grated Parmesan cheese

¼ teaspoon paprika

¼ teaspoon garlic powder

½ teaspoon dried thyme

1 tablespoon all-purpose flour

DIRECTIONS

1 Preheat the air fryer to 380 degrees.

2 In a medium bowl, stir together the Parmesan, paprika, garlic powder, thyme, and flour.

3 Line the air fryer basket with parchment paper.

4 Using a tablespoon measuring tool, create 1-tablespoon mounds of seasoned cheese on the parchment paper, leaving 2 inches between the mounds to allow for spreading.

5 Cook the crackers for 6 minutes. Allow the cheese to harden and cool before handling. Repeat in batches with the remaining cheese.

TIP: Buy shredded cheese to make these chips in an instant!

VARY IT! Add in ¼ cup finely grated cheddar for simple cheddar bites.

Plantain Chips

PREP TIME: 10 MIN	COOK TIME: 14 MIN	YIELD: 2 SERVINGS

INGREDIENTS

1 large green plantain

2½ cups filtered water, divided

2 teaspoons sea salt, divided

DIRECTIONS

1 Slice the plantain into 1-inch pieces. Place the plantains into a large bowl, cover with 2 cups water and 1 teaspoon salt. Soak the plantains for 30 minutes; then remove and pat dry.

2 Preheat the air fryer to 390 degrees.

3 Place the plantain pieces into the air fryer basket, leaving space between the plantain rounds. Cook the plantains for 5 minutes, and carefully remove them from the air fryer basket.

4 Add the remaining water to a small bowl.

5 Using a small drinking glass, dip the bottom of the glass into the water and mash the warm plantains until they're ¼-inch thick. Return the plantains to the air fryer basket, sprinkle with the remaining sea salt, and spray lightly with cooking spray.

6 Cook for another 6 to 8 minutes, or until lightly golden brown edges appear.

NOTE: Plantains are members of the banana family, but they have more fiber, more starch, and much less sugar.

TIP: Serve with fresh guacamole or a bowl of rice and beans.

VARY IT! You can also make these chips sweet. Instead of salt, sprinkle the plantain rounds with sugar. For a fun twist, try slicing the plantain lengthwise instead of into rounds.

Root Vegetable Crisps

INGREDIENTS

1 small taro root, peeled and washed

1 small yucca root, peeled and washed

1 small purple sweet potato, washed

2 cups filtered water

2 teaspoons extra-virgin olive oil

½ teaspoon salt

DIRECTIONS

1 Using a mandolin, slice the taro root, yucca root, and purple sweet potato into ⅛-inch slices.

2 Add the water to a large bowl. Add the sliced vegetables and soak for at least 30 minutes.

3 Preheat the air fryer to 370 degrees.

4 Drain the water and pat the vegetables dry with a paper towel or kitchen cloth. Toss the vegetables with the olive oil and sprinkle with salt. Liberally spray the air fryer basket with olive oil mist.

5 Place the vegetables into the air fryer basket, making sure not to overlap the pieces.

6 Cook for 8 minutes, shaking the basket every 2 minutes, until the outer edges start to turn up and the vegetables start to brown. Remove from the basket and serve warm. Repeat with the remaining vegetable slices until all are cooked.

NOTE: Depending on the size of your air fryer, you may need to cook in multiple batches.

TIP: You may need to adjust the cooking time depending on how hot your air fryer gets. Keep a close eye on the chips to prevent burning them.

VARY IT! Want to jazz them up? Consider sprinkling them with a teaspoon or two of one of the spice blends from Chapter 2.

Sweet Potato Chips

PREP TIME: 40 MIN	COOK TIME: 10 MIN	YIELD: 4 SERVINGS

INGREDIENTS

2 medium sweet potatoes, washed

2 cups filtered water

1 tablespoon avocado oil

2 teaspoons brown sugar

½ teaspoon salt

DIRECTIONS

1 Using a mandolin, slice the potatoes into ⅛-inch pieces.

2 Add the water to a large bowl. Place the potatoes in the bowl, and soak for at least 30 minutes.

3 Preheat the air fryer to 350 degrees.

4 Drain the water and pat the chips dry with a paper towel or kitchen cloth. Toss the chips with the avocado oil, brown sugar, and salt. Liberally spray the air fryer basket with olive oil mist.

5 Set the chips inside the air fryer, separating them so they're not on top of each other. Cook for 5 minutes, shake the basket, and cook another 5 minutes, or until browned.

6 Remove and let cool a few minutes prior to serving. Repeat until all the chips are cooked.

VARY IT! Prefer a little spice? Omit the brown sugar and use smoked paprika or chili powder instead.

Chapter 11

Meaty Mains

T hink the air fryer is just to make your favorite "fried" foods fast? Think again!

This chapter opens your eyes to the culinary delights that can come out of your air fryer. From Beef Short Ribs to Chicken Souvlaki Gyros, there's a meaty main in this chapter that will appeal to every carnivore.

Be sure to check out Chapter 9 and plan enough time to create a drool-worthy side to accompany your main meal. Trust us, you'll thank us later when you pair the Parmesan Garlic Fries (Chapter 9) with the Steakhouse Burgers in this chapter!

Rosemary Lamb Chops

PREP TIME: 12 MIN	COOK TIME: 6 MIN	YIELD: 4 SERVINGS

INGREDIENTS

8 lamb chops

1 tablespoon extra-virgin olive oil

1 teaspoon dried rosemary, crushed

2 cloves garlic, minced

1 teaspoon sea salt

¼ teaspoon black pepper

DIRECTIONS

1 In a large bowl, mix together the lamb chops, olive oil, rosemary, garlic, salt, and pepper. Let sit at room temperature for 10 minutes.

2 Meanwhile, preheat the air fryer to 380 degrees.

3 Cook the lamb chops for 3 minutes, flip them over, and cook for another 3 minutes.

NOTE: If the lamb chops are thin, cut the time to 4 minutes total and check for an internal temperature of 145 degrees.

TIP: Serve over a bed of spicy greens like arugula, kale, or spinach.

VARY IT! Try different herbs or spices, like thyme, coriander, or parsley.

Beef Short Ribs

PREP TIME: 1 HR	COOK TIME: 20 MIN	YIELD: 4 SERVINGS

INGREDIENTS

2 tablespoons soy sauce

1 tablespoon sesame oil

2 tablespoons brown sugar

1 teaspoon ground ginger

2 garlic cloves, crushed

1 pound beef short ribs

DIRECTIONS

1 In a small bowl, mix together the soy sauce, sesame oil, brown sugar, and ginger. Transfer the mixture to a large resealable plastic bag, and place the garlic cloves and short ribs into the bag. Secure and place in the refrigerator for an hour (or overnight).

2 When you're ready to prepare the dish, preheat the air fryer to 330 degrees.

3 Liberally spray the air fryer basket with olive oil mist and set the beef short ribs in the basket.

4 Cook for 10 minutes, flip the short ribs, and then cook another 10 minutes.

5 Remove the short ribs from the air fryer basket, loosely cover with aluminum foil, and let them rest. The short ribs will continue to cook after they're removed from the basket. Check the internal temperature after 5 minutes to make sure it reached 145 degrees if you prefer a well-done meat. If it didn't reach 145 degrees and you would like it to be cooked longer, you can put it back into the air fryer basket at 330 degrees for another 3 minutes.

6 Remove from the basket and let it rest, covered with aluminum foil, for 5 minutes. Serve immediately.

NOTE: If you prefer more of a rare meat, decrease the cooking time to 14 minutes total.

TIP: Pair with Crispy Herbed Potatoes (Chapter 9) and a side salad.

Mustard-Crusted Rib-Eye

PREP TIME: 35 MIN	COOK TIME: 9 MIN	YIELD: 2 SERVINGS

INGREDIENTS

Two 6-ounce rib-eye steaks, about 1-inch thick

1 teaspoon coarse salt

½ teaspoon coarse black pepper

2 tablespoons Dijon mustard

DIRECTIONS

1 Rub the steaks with the salt and pepper. Then spread the mustard on both sides of the steaks. Cover with foil and let the steaks sit at room temperature for 30 minutes.

2 Preheat the air fryer to 390 degrees.

3 Cook the steaks for 9 minutes. Check for an internal temperature of 140 degrees and immediately remove the steaks and let them rest for 5 minutes before slicing.

NOTE: Using a thermometer is the most accurate way to ensure that your meat is not over- or undercooked.

TIP: Sirloin steaks are a leaner cut. If you opt for a sirloin, you'll need to reduce the cooking time.

VARY IT! Try this dish with any of your favorite steak seasonings.

Steakhouse Burgers with Red Onion Compote

PREP TIME: 20 MIN	COOK TIME: 22 MIN	YIELD: 4 SERVINGS

INGREDIENTS

1½ pounds lean ground beef

2 cloves garlic, minced and divided

1 teaspoon Worcestershire sauce

1 teaspoon sea salt, divided

½ teaspoon black pepper

1 tablespoon extra-virgin olive oil

1 red onion, thinly sliced

¼ cup balsamic vinegar

1 teaspoon sugar

1 tablespoon tomato paste

2 tablespoons mayonnaise

2 tablespoons sour cream

4 brioche hamburger buns

1 cup arugula

DIRECTIONS

1 In a large bowl, mix together the ground beef, 1 of the minced garlic cloves, the Worcestershire sauce, ½ teaspoon of the salt, and the black pepper. Form the meat into 1-inch-thick patties. Make a dent in the center (this helps the center cook evenly). Let the meat sit for 15 minutes.

2 Meanwhile, in a small saucepan over medium heat, cook the olive oil and red onion for 4 minutes, stirring frequently to avoid burning. Add in the balsamic vinegar, sugar, and tomato paste, and cook for an additional 3 minutes, stirring frequently. Transfer the onion compote to a small bowl.

3 Preheat the air fryer to 350 degrees.

4 In another small bowl, mix together the remaining minced garlic, the mayonnaise, and the sour cream. Spread the mayo mixture on the insides of the brioche buns.

5 Cook the hamburgers for 6 minutes, flip the burgers, and cook an additional 2 to 6 minutes. Check the internal temperature to avoid under- or overcooking. Hamburgers should be cooked to at least 160 degrees. After cooking, cover with foil and let the meat rest for 5 minutes.

6 Meanwhile, place the buns inside the air fryer and toast them for 3 minutes.

7 To assemble the burgers, place the hamburger on one side of the bun, top with onion compote and ¼ cup arugula, and then place the other half of the bun on top.

NOTE: From a food safety perspective, we always advise cooking red meat to medium or well done.

TIP: Use a mandolin on the thinnest setting to get paper-thin onions.

NOTE: Serve with a tossed salad and air-fried potatoes.

Peppered Steak Bites

PREP TIME: 5 MIN	COOK TIME: 14 MIN	YIELD: 4 SERVINGS

INGREDIENTS

1 pound sirloin steak, cut into 1-inch cubes

½ teaspoon coarse sea salt

1 teaspoon coarse black pepper

2 teaspoons Worcestershire sauce

½ teaspoon garlic powder

¼ teaspoon red pepper flakes

¼ cup chopped parsley

DIRECTIONS

1 Preheat the air fryer to 390 degrees.

2 In a large bowl, place the steak cubes and toss with the salt, pepper, Worcestershire sauce, garlic powder, and red pepper flakes.

3 Pour the steak into the air fryer basket and cook for 10 to 14 minutes, depending on how well done you prefer your bites. Starting at the 8-minute mark, toss the steak bites every 2 minutes to check for doneness.

4 When the steak is cooked, remove it from the basket to a serving bowl and top with the chopped parsley. Allow the steak to rest for 5 minutes before serving.

TIP: If you prefer a richer flavor, toss the steak with 1 tablespoon of melted butter after cooking.

VARY IT! Love short ribs? Opt for a boneless short rib and thinly slice instead of into cubes.

VARY IT! You can cut costs and add nutrition by cutting the meat in half and adding 6 ounces of mushrooms.

Beef al Carbon (Street Taco Meat)

PREP TIME: 35 MIN	COOK TIME: 8 MIN	YIELD: 6 SERVINGS

INGREDIENTS

1½ pounds sirloin steak, cut into ½-inch cubes

¾ cup lime juice

½ cup extra-virgin olive oil

1 teaspoon ground cumin

2 teaspoons garlic powder

1 teaspoon salt

DIRECTIONS

1 In a large bowl, toss together the steak, lime juice, olive oil, cumin, garlic powder, and salt. Allow the meat to marinate for 30 minutes. Drain off all the marinade and pat the meat dry with paper towels.

2 Preheat the air fryer to 400 degrees.

3 Place the meat in the air fryer basket and spray with cooking spray. Cook the meat for 5 minutes, toss the meat, and continue cooking another 3 minutes, until slightly crispy.

NOTE: These are different from fajitas or carne asada, which is typically cooked steak. Street tacos are often chopped meat that have crispy bits.

TIP: Serve the meat in heated corn tortillas with chopped cilantro and onion or on top of your favorite bed of greens for a festive salad.

VARY IT! Whip up a quick and spicy crema with sour cream, lime juice, and your favorite hot sauce. Drizzle on top for a spicy finish.

California Burritos

INGREDIENTS

1 pound sirloin steak, sliced thin

1 teaspoon dried oregano

1 teaspoon ground cumin

½ teaspoon garlic powder

16 tater tots

⅓ cup sour cream

½ lime, juiced

2 tablespoons hot sauce

1 large avocado, pitted

1 teaspoon salt, divided

4 large (8- to 10-inch) flour tortillas

½ cup shredded cheddar cheese or Monterey jack

2 tablespoons avocado oil

DIRECTIONS

1 Preheat the air fryer to 380 degrees.

2 Season the steak with oregano, cumin, and garlic powder. Place the steak on one side of the air fryer and the tater tots on the other side. (It's okay for them to touch, because the flavors will all come together in the burrito.) Cook for 8 minutes, toss, and cook an additional 4 to 6 minutes.

3 Meanwhile, in a small bowl, stir together the sour cream, lime juice, and hot sauce.

4 In another small bowl, mash together the avocado and season with ½ teaspoon of the salt, to taste.

5 To assemble the burrito, lay out the tortillas, equally divide the meat amongst the tortillas. Season the steak equally with the remaining ½ teaspoon salt. Then layer the mashed avocado and sour cream mixture on top. Top each tortilla with 4 tater tots and finish each with 2 tablespoons cheese. Roll up the sides and, while holding in the sides, roll up the burrito. Place the burritos in the air fryer basket and brush with avocado oil (working in batches as needed); cook for 3 minutes or until lightly golden on the outside.

NOTE: Traditional California burritos have french fries instead of tater tots, but when recipe testing, we found that tater tots were a space saver in cooking both the meat and the potatoes together. If you have fries on hand, feel free to make a swap.

TIP: Serve these hearty burritos with a salad to complete the meal.

VARY IT! Lighten it up by using plain Greek yogurt instead of sour cream.

Indian Fry Bread Tacos

PREP TIME: 20 MIN	COOK TIME: 20 MIN	YIELD: 4 SERVINGS

INGREDIENTS

1 cup all-purpose flour

1½ teaspoons salt, divided

1½ teaspoons baking powder

¼ cup milk

¼ cup warm water

½ pound lean ground beef

One 14.5-ounce can pinto beans, drained and rinsed

1 tablespoon taco seasoning

½ cup shredded cheddar cheese

2 cups shredded lettuce

¼ cup black olives, chopped

1 Roma tomato, diced

1 avocado, diced

1 lime

DIRECTIONS

1 In a large bowl, whisk together the flour, 1 teaspoon of the salt, and baking powder. Make a well in the center and add in the milk and water. Form a ball and gently knead the dough four times. Cover the bowl with a damp towel, and set aside.

2 Preheat the air fryer to 380 degrees.

3 In a medium bowl, mix together the ground beef, beans, and taco seasoning. Crumble the meat mixture into the air fryer basket and cook for 5 minutes; toss the meat and cook an additional 2 to 3 minutes, or until cooked fully. Place the cooked meat in a bowl for taco assembly; season with the remaining ½ teaspoon salt as desired.

4 On a floured surface, place the dough. Cut the dough into 4 equal parts. Using a rolling pin, roll out each piece of dough to 5 inches in diameter. Spray the dough with cooking spray and place in the air fryer basket, working in batches as needed. Cook for 3 minutes, flip over, spray with cooking spray, and cook for an additional 1 to 3 minutes, until golden and puffy.

5 To assemble, place the fry breads on a serving platter. Equally divide the meat and bean mixture on top of the fry bread. Divide the cheese, lettuce, olives, tomatoes, and avocado among the four tacos. Squeeze lime over the top prior to serving.

NOTE: Fry breads are typically not picked up like a traditional Mexican taco; instead, you can serve them open faced and pick them up to eat or use a fork and knife.

TIP: This dough recipe is incredibly versatile. Brush it with olive oil and garlic powder and serve it as a side dish instead if you like.

VARY IT! Taco toppings can be fun and creative. You can make breakfast fry bread with scrambled eggs, potatoes, and bacon.

Asian Meatball Tacos

PREP TIME: 20 MIN	COOK TIME: 10 MIN	YIELD: 4 SERVINGS

INGREDIENTS

1 pound lean ground turkey

3 tablespoons soy sauce

1 tablespoon brown sugar

½ teaspoon onion powder

½ teaspoon garlic powder

1 tablespoon sesame seeds

1 English cucumber

4 radishes

2 tablespoons white wine vinegar

1 lime, juiced and divided

1 tablespoon avocado oil

Salt, to taste

½ cup Greek yogurt

1 to 3 teaspoons Sriracha, based on desired spiciness

1 cup shredded cabbage

¼ cup chopped cilantro

Eight 6-inch flour tortillas

DIRECTIONS

1 Preheat the air fryer to 360 degrees.

2 In a large bowl, mix the ground turkey, soy sauce, brown sugar, onion powder, garlic powder, and sesame seeds. Form the meat into 1-inch meatballs and place in the air fryer basket. Cook for 5 minutes, shake the basket, and cook another 5 minutes. Using a food thermometer, make sure the internal temperature of the meatballs is 165 degrees.

3 Meanwhile, dice the cucumber and radishes and place in a medium bowl. Add the white wine vinegar, 1 teaspoon of the lime juice, and the avocado oil, and stir to coat. Season with salt to desired taste.

4 In a large bowl, mix the Greek yogurt, Sriracha, and the remaining lime juice, and stir. Add in the cabbage and cilantro; toss well to create a slaw.

5 In a heavy skillet, heat the tortillas over medium heat for 1 to 2 minutes on each side, or until warmed.

6 To serve, place a tortilla on a plate, top with 5 meatballs, then with cucumber and radish salad, and finish with 2 tablespoons of cabbage slaw.

TIP: Invest in a food thermometer to ensure meats or casserole dishes are cooked completely.

VARY IT! Prefer beef? Swap out ground turkey with beef instead.

Italian Meatballs

PREP TIME: 15 MIN | COOK TIME: 12 MIN | YIELD: 4 SERVINGS

INGREDIENTS

12 ounces lean ground beef

4 ounces Italian sausage, casing removed

½ cup breadcrumbs

1 cup grated Parmesan cheese

1 egg

2 tablespoons milk

2 teaspoons Italian seasoning

½ teaspoon onion powder

½ teaspoon garlic powder

Pinch of red pepper flakes

DIRECTIONS

1 In a large bowl, place all the ingredients and mix well. Roll out 24 meatballs.

2 Preheat the air fryer to 360 degrees.

3 Place the meatballs in the air fryer basket and cook for 12 minutes, tossing every 4 minutes. Using a food thermometer, check to ensure the internal temperature of the meatballs is 165 degrees.

TIP: Serve these meatballs in a toasted bun, on a Greek salad, or mixed with a marinara sauce over fresh pasta.

TIP: After cooking the meatballs, place them on a plate and stick them in the freezer. Once frozen, transfer to a freezer-safe bag and store for up to 6 months. You can reheat frozen meatballs at 380 degrees for 9 minutes, being sure to check the internal temperature prior to serving.

Prosciutto and Arugula Personal Pizzas

PREP TIME: 10 MIN	COOK TIME: 10 MIN	YIELD: 4 SERVINGS

INGREDIENTS

One 12-inch pizza dough

½ cup marinara sauce

2 ounces prosciutto, chopped

1 cup grated mozzarella cheese

2 cups arugula

½ lemon, juiced

1 tablespoon extra-virgin olive oil

⅛ teaspoon salt

¼ teaspoon black pepper

DIRECTIONS

1 On a floured surface, cut the dough ball into quarters. Roll each dough ball out to 4-inch rounds (to form a thin crust).

2 Preheat the air fryer to 370 degrees.

3 Top each pizza with 2 tablespoons marinara, ½ ounce prosciutto, and 4 tablespoons mozzarella cheese.

4 Spray the air fryer basket with cooking spray. Depending on the size of your air fryer basket, cook 1 or 2 pizzas at a time for 7 minutes each, or until the cheese is melted and beginning to be golden.

5 Meanwhile, in a medium bowl, toss together the arugula and lemon juice, gently squeezing the greens. Add the olive oil, salt, and pepper, and taste for seasoning.

6 To serve, place ½ cup greens on each individual pizza.

TIP: If your pizza is browning too quickly, reduce the temperature to 350 degrees and cook for 10 minutes or until done.

VARY IT! Keep it vegetarian and use fresh mushrooms instead of prosciutto.

Chicken Adobo

PREP TIME: 1 HR | **COOK TIME: 12 MIN** | **YIELD: 6 SERVINGS**

INGREDIENTS

6 boneless chicken thighs

¼ cup soy sauce or tamari

½ cup rice wine vinegar

4 cloves garlic, minced

⅛ teaspoon crushed red pepper flakes

½ teaspoon black pepper

DIRECTIONS

1 Place the chicken thighs into a resealable plastic bag with the soy sauce or tamari, the rice wine vinegar, the garlic, and the crushed red pepper flakes. Seal the bag and let the chicken marinate at least 1 hour in the refrigerator.

2 Preheat the air fryer to 400 degrees.

3 Drain the chicken and pat dry with a paper towel. Season the chicken with black pepper and liberally spray with cooking spray.

4 Place the chicken in the air fryer basket and cook for 9 minutes, turn over at 9 minutes and check for an internal temperature of 165 degrees, and cook another 3 minutes.

TIP: Serve with steamed rice and steamed green beans to complete the meal.

Sweet-and-Sour Chicken

PREP TIME: 15 MIN   **COOK TIME: 10 MIN**   **YIELD: 6 SERVINGS**

INGREDIENTS

1 cup pineapple juice

1 cup plus 3 tablespoons cornstarch, divided

¼ cup sugar

¼ cup ketchup

¼ cup apple cider vinegar

2 tablespoons soy sauce or tamari

1 teaspoon garlic powder, divided

¼ cup flour

1 tablespoon sesame seeds

½ teaspoon salt

¼ teaspoon ground black pepper

2 large eggs

2 pounds chicken breasts, cut into 1-inch cubes

1 red bell pepper, cut into 1-inch pieces

1 carrot, sliced into ¼-inch-thick rounds

DIRECTIONS

1   In a medium saucepan, whisk together the pineapple juice, 3 tablespoons of the cornstarch, the sugar, the ketchup, the apple cider vinegar, the soy sauce or tamari, and ½ teaspoon of the garlic powder. Cook over medium-low heat, whisking occasionally as the sauce thickens, about 6 minutes. Stir and set aside while preparing the chicken.

2   Preheat the air fryer to 370 degrees.

3   In a medium bowl, place the remaining 1 cup of cornstarch, the flour, the sesame seeds, the salt, the remaining ½ teaspoon of garlic powder, and the pepper.

4   In a second medium bowl, whisk the eggs.

5   Working in batches, place the cubed chicken in the cornstarch mixture to lightly coat; then dip it into the egg mixture, and return it to the cornstarch mixture. Shake off the excess and place the coated chicken in the air fryer basket. Spray with cooking spray and cook for 5 minutes, shake the basket, and spray with more cooking spray. Cook an additional 3 to 5 minutes, or until completely cooked and golden brown.

6   On the last batch of chicken, add the bell pepper and carrot to the basket and cook with the chicken.

7   Place the cooked chicken and vegetables into a serving bowl and toss with the sweet-and-sour sauce to serve.

TIP: Serve with steamed rice or on a bed of shredded cabbage.

VARY IT! Add in more vegetables, like broccoli, zucchini, or onions, if you like.

Crispy "Fried" Chicken

| PREP TIME: 20 MIN | COOK TIME: 14 MIN | YIELD: 4 SERVINGS |

INGREDIENTS

¾ cup all-purpose flour

½ teaspoon paprika

¼ teaspoon black pepper

¼ teaspoon salt

2 large eggs

1½ cups panko breadcrumbs

1 pound boneless, skinless chicken tenders

DIRECTIONS

1 Preheat the air fryer to 400 degrees.

2 In a shallow bowl, mix the flour with the paprika, pepper, and salt.

3 In a separate bowl, whisk the eggs; set aside.

4 In a third bowl, place the breadcrumbs.

5 Liberally spray the air fryer basket with olive oil spray.

6 Pat the chicken tenders dry with a paper towel. Dredge the tenders one at a time in the flour, then dip them in the egg, and toss them in the breadcrumb coating. Repeat until all tenders are coated.

7 Set each tender in the air fryer, leaving room on each side of the tender to allow for flipping.

8 When the basket is full, cook 4 to 7 minutes, flip, and cook another 4 to 7 minutes.

9 Remove the tenders and let cool 5 minutes before serving. Repeat until all tenders are cooked.

NOTE: Use a thermometer to check the internal temperature of the chicken. It should read 165 degrees. Drop-basket air fryers tend to cook these in 8 minutes, as opposed to the conventional oven style with a door, which can take up to 14 minutes.

TIP: Serve with your favorite dipping sauce, like ranch, honey mustard, or barbecue sauce.

VARY IT! Prefer a little cheesy twist? Add ¼ cup of grated Parmesan cheese to the breadcrumbs.

Southern-Style Chicken Legs

PREP TIME: 4 HR	COOK TIME: 20 MIN	YIELD: 6 SERVINGS

INGREDIENTS

2 cups buttermilk

1 tablespoon hot sauce

12 chicken legs

½ teaspoon salt

½ teaspoon pepper

1 teaspoon paprika

½ teaspoon onion powder

1 teaspoon garlic powder

1 cup all-purpose flour

DIRECTIONS

1 In an airtight container, place the buttermilk, hot sauce, and chicken legs and refrigerate for 4 to 8 hours.

2 In a medium bowl, whisk together the salt, pepper, paprika, onion powder, garlic powder, and flour. Drain the chicken legs from the buttermilk and dip the chicken legs into the flour mixture, stirring to coat well.

3 Preheat the air fryer to 390 degrees.

4 Place the chicken legs in the air fryer basket and spray with cooking spray. Cook for 10 minutes, turn the chicken legs over, and cook for another 8 to 10 minutes. Check for an internal temperature of 165 degrees.

TIP: Serve the drumsticks with potato salad and steamed broccoli for a complete meal. Splash on some hot sauce for a spicy kick.

Gluten-Free Nutty Chicken Fingers

PREP TIME: 20 MIN	COOK TIME: 10 MIN	YIELD: 4 SERVINGS

INGREDIENTS

½ cup gluten-free flour

½ teaspoon garlic powder

¼ teaspoon onion powder

¼ teaspoon black pepper

¼ teaspoon salt

1 cup walnuts, pulsed into coarse flour

½ cup gluten-free breadcrumbs

2 large eggs

1 pound boneless, skinless chicken tenders

DIRECTIONS

1 Preheat the air fryer to 400 degrees.

2 In a medium bowl, mix the flour, garlic, onion, pepper, and salt. Set aside.

3 In a separate bowl, mix the walnut flour and breadcrumbs.

4 In a third bowl, whisk the eggs.

5 Liberally spray the air fryer basket with olive oil spray.

6 Pat the chicken tenders dry with a paper towel. Dredge the tenders one at a time in the flour, then dip them in the egg, and toss them in the breadcrumb coating. Repeat until all tenders are coated.

7 Set each tender in the air fryer, leaving room on each side of the tender to allow for flipping.

8 When the basket is full, cook 5 minutes, flip, and cook another 5 minutes. Check the internal temperature after cooking completes; it should read 165 degrees. If it does not, cook another 2 to 4 minutes.

9 Remove the tenders and let cool 5 minutes before serving. Repeat until all the tenders are cooked.

NOTE: Use a thermometer to check the internal temperature of the chicken. It should read 165 degrees. Drop-basket air fryers tend to cook these in 8 minutes versus the conventional oven style with the door, which can take up to 14 minutes.

TIP: Serve with a honey mustard sauce or place on top of your favorite salad.

TIP: Make your own gluten-free breadcrumbs using gluten-free bread. In Chapter 9, you can make the croutons in the Panzanella Salad with Crispy Croutons recipe.

VARY IT! Have another nut on hand? Swap them in for the walnuts and experience a unique flavor profile!

Chicken Cordon Bleu

PREP TIME: 15 MIN | **COOK TIME: 16 MIN** | **YIELD: 2 SERVINGS**

INGREDIENTS

2 boneless, skinless chicken breasts

¼ teaspoon salt

2 teaspoons Dijon mustard

2 ounces deli ham

2 ounces Swiss, fontina, or Gruyère cheese

⅓ cup all-purpose flour

1 egg

½ cup breadcrumbs

DIRECTIONS

1 Pat the chicken breasts with a paper towel. Season the chicken with the salt. Pound the chicken breasts to 1½ inches thick. Create a pouch by slicing the side of each chicken breast. Spread 1 teaspoon Dijon mustard inside the pouch of each chicken breast. Wrap a 1-ounce slice of ham around a 1-ounce slice of cheese and place into the pouch. Repeat with the remaining ham and cheese.

2 In a medium bowl, place the flour.

3 In a second bowl, whisk the egg.

4 In a third bowl, place the breadcrumbs.

5 Dredge the chicken in the flour and shake off the excess. Next, dip the chicken into the egg and then in the breadcrumbs. Set the chicken on a plate and repeat with the remaining chicken piece.

6 Preheat the air fryer to 360 degrees.

7 Place the chicken in the air fryer basket and spray liberally with cooking spray. Cook for 8 minutes, turn the chicken breasts over, and liberally spray with cooking spray again; cook another 6 minutes. Once golden brown, check for an internal temperature of 165 degrees.

TIP: Serve with steamed green beans and roasted potatoes for a complete meal.

Chicken Souvlaki Gyros

PREP TIME: 2 HR 5 MIN	COOK TIME: 18 MIN	YIELD: 4 SERVINGS

INGREDIENTS

¼ cup extra-virgin olive oil

1 clove garlic, crushed

1 tablespoon Italian seasoning

½ teaspoon paprika

½ lemon, sliced

¼ teaspoon salt

1 pound boneless, skinless chicken breasts

4 whole-grain pita breads

1 cup shredded lettuce

½ cup chopped tomatoes

¼ cup chopped red onion

¼ cup cucumber yogurt sauce

DIRECTIONS

1 In a large resealable plastic bag, combine the olive oil, garlic, Italian seasoning, paprika, lemon, and salt. Add the chicken to the bag and secure shut. Vigorously shake until all the ingredients are combined. Set in the fridge for 2 hours to marinate.

2 When ready to cook, preheat the air fryer to 360 degrees.

3 Liberally spray the air fryer basket with olive oil mist. Remove the chicken from the bag and discard the leftover marinade. Place the chicken into the air fryer basket, allowing enough room between the chicken breasts to flip.

4 Cook for 10 minutes, flip, and cook another 8 minutes.

5 Remove the chicken from the air fryer basket when it has cooked (or the internal temperature of the chicken reaches 165 degrees). Let rest 5 minutes. Then thinly slice the chicken into strips.

6 Assemble the gyros by placing the pita bread on a flat surface and topping with chicken, lettuce, tomatoes, onion, and a drizzle of yogurt sauce.

7 Serve warm.

NOTE: Do not marinate more than 2 hours with the lemon inside.

TIP: Warm the pita bread in the air fryer for a minute for a restaurant-like feel.

Crispy Chicken Parmesan

PREP TIME: 15 MIN	COOK TIME: 12 MIN	YIELD: 4 SERVINGS

INGREDIENTS

4 skinless, boneless chicken breasts, pounded thin to ¼-inch thickness

1 teaspoon salt, divided

½ teaspoon black pepper, divided

1 cup flour

2 eggs

1 cup panko breadcrumbs

½ teaspoon dried oregano

½ cup grated Parmesan cheese

DIRECTIONS

1 Pat the chicken breasts with a paper towel. Season the chicken with ½ teaspoon of the salt and ¼ teaspoon of the pepper.

2 In a medium bowl, place the flour.

3 In a second bowl, whisk the eggs.

4 In a third bowl, place the breadcrumbs, oregano, cheese, and the remaining ½ teaspoon of salt and ¼ teaspoon of pepper.

5 Dredge the chicken in the flour and shake off the excess. Dip the chicken into the eggs and then into the breadcrumbs. Set the chicken on a plate and repeat with the remaining chicken pieces.

6 Preheat the air fryer to 360 degrees.

7 Place the chicken in the air fryer basket and spray liberally with cooking spray. Cook for 8 minutes, turn the chicken breasts over, and cook another 4 minutes. When golden brown, check for an internal temperature of 165 degrees.

TIP: Serve with fresh marinara and pasta.

Mediterranean Stuffed Chicken Breasts

PREP TIME: 15 MIN	COOK TIME: 24 MIN	YIELD: 4 SERVINGS

INGREDIENTS

4 boneless, skinless chicken breasts

½ teaspoon salt

½ teaspoon black pepper

½ teaspoon garlic powder

½ teaspoon paprika

½ cup canned artichoke hearts, chopped

4 ounces cream cheese

¼ cup grated Parmesan cheese

DIRECTIONS

1 Pat the chicken breasts with a paper towel. Using a sharp knife, cut a pouch in the side of each chicken breast for filling.

2 In a small bowl, mix the salt, pepper, garlic powder, and paprika. Season the chicken breasts with this mixture.

3 In a medium bowl, mix together the artichokes, cream cheese, and grated Parmesan cheese. Divide the filling between the 4 breasts, stuffing it inside the pouches. Use toothpicks to close the pouches and secure the filling.

4 Preheat the air fryer to 360 degrees.

5 Spray the air fryer basket liberally with cooking spray, add the stuffed chicken breasts to the basket, and spray liberally with cooking spray again. Cook for 14 minutes, carefully turn over the chicken breasts, and cook another 10 minutes. Check the temperature at 20 minutes cooking. Chicken breasts are fully cooked when the center measures 165 degrees. Cook in batches, if needed.

NOTE: Stuffed meats take longer to cook due to the filling. If the meat is getting too brown, reduce the air fryer temperature to 330 degrees and continue cooking until fully cooked.

TIP: Serve with orzo pasta and steamed asparagus to complete the meal.

VARY IT! Prefer cheddar? Use grated cheddar cheese in place of the Parmesan, and season the chicken breasts with ranch seasoning.

Italian Roasted Chicken Thighs

PREP TIME: 5 MIN	COOK TIME: 14 MIN	YIELD: 6 SERVINGS

INGREDIENTS

6 boneless chicken thighs

½ teaspoon dried oregano

½ teaspoon garlic powder

½ teaspoon sea salt

½ teaspoon black pepper

¼ teaspoon crushed red pepper flakes

DIRECTIONS

1 Pat the chicken thighs with paper towel.

2 In a small bowl, mix the oregano, garlic powder, salt, pepper, and crushed red pepper flakes. Rub the spice mixture onto the chicken thighs.

3 Preheat the air fryer to 400 degrees.

4 Place the chicken thighs in the air fryer basket and spray with cooking spray. Cook for 10 minutes, turn over, and cook another 4 minutes. When cooking completes, the internal temperature should read 165 degrees.

TIP: Serve with sautéed asparagus and couscous.

VARY IT! Try a lemon-pepper or garlic-and-rosemary rub instead.

Chicken Tikka

PREP TIME: 40 MIN	COOK TIME: 15 MIN	YIELD: 4 SERVINGS

INGREDIENTS

¼ cup plain Greek yogurt

1 clove garlic, minced

1 tablespoon ketchup

1 tablespoon extra-virgin olive oil

1 tablespoon lemon juice

½ teaspoon salt

½ teaspoon ground cumin

½ teaspoon paprika

¼ teaspoon ground cinnamon

½ teaspoon ground black pepper

½ teaspoon cayenne pepper

1 pound boneless, skinless chicken thighs

DIRECTIONS

1 In a large bowl, stir together the yogurt, garlic, ketchup, olive oil, lemon juice, salt, cumin, paprika, cinnamon, black pepper, and cayenne pepper until combined.

2 Add the chicken thighs to the bow and fold the yogurt-spice mixture over the chicken thighs until they're covered with the marinade. Cover with plastic wrap and place in the refrigerator for 30 minutes.

3 When ready to cook the chicken, remove from the refrigerator and preheat the air fryer to 370 degrees.

4 Liberally spray the air fryer basket with olive oil mist. Place the chicken thighs into the air fryer basket, leaving space between the thighs to turn.

5 Cook for 10 minutes, turn the chicken thighs, and cook another 5 minutes (or until the internal temperature reaches 165 degrees).

6 Remove the chicken from the air fryer and serve warm with desired sides.

NOTE: If you have air-fryer-compatible skewers, you can cube the thighs and cook them on the skewers. You can also add bell peppers and onions to the skewers to create a more robust meal and serve over rice.

TIP: This recipe pairs great with a cucumber yogurt salad and warm lavash bread.

Chicken Flautas

PREP TIME: 10 MIN	COOK TIME: 8 MIN	YIELD: 6 SERVINGS

INGREDIENTS

6 tablespoons whipped cream cheese

1 cup shredded cooked chicken

6 tablespoons mild pico de gallo salsa

⅓ cup shredded Mexican cheese

½ teaspoon taco seasoning

Six 8-inch flour tortillas

2 cups shredded lettuce

½ cup guacamole

DIRECTIONS

1 Preheat the air fryer to 370 degrees.

2 In a large bowl, mix the cream cheese, chicken, salsa, shredded cheese, and taco seasoning until well combined.

3 Lay the tortillas on a flat surface. Divide the cheese-and-chicken mixture into 6 equal portions; then place the mixture in the center of the tortillas, spreading evenly, leaving about 1 inch from the edge of the tortilla.

4 Spray the air fryer basket with olive oil spray. Roll up the flautas and place them edge side down into the basket. Lightly mist the top of the flautas with olive oil spray.

5 Repeat until the air fryer basket is full. You may need to cook these in batches, depending on the size of your air fryer.

6 Cook for 7 minutes, or until the outer edges are browned.

7 Remove from the air fryer basket and serve warm over a bed of shredded lettuce with guacamole on top.

NOTE: You can make these flautas using corn tortillas, which would be more of a taquito, but the corn tortillas tend to crumble more when rolling. Be sure to warm them prior to assembling if you choose to make them with the corn.

TIP: Using a whipped cream cheese makes it easier to assemble the mixture. You can whip your own cream cheese by using a hand mixer. Essentially, this is just whipping air into the cream cheese.

VARY IT! Swap in your favorite protein of choice or make them vegetarian by using a black bean and corn salsa.

Jerk Turkey Meatballs

PREP TIME: 10 MIN	COOK TIME: 8 MIN	YIELD: 7 SERVINGS

INGREDIENTS

1 pound lean ground turkey

¼ cup chopped onion

1 teaspoon minced garlic

½ teaspoon dried thyme

¼ teaspoon ground cinnamon

1 teaspoon cayenne pepper

½ teaspoon paprika

½ teaspoon salt

⅛ teaspoon black pepper

¼ teaspoon red pepper flakes

2 teaspoons brown sugar

1 large egg, whisked

⅓ cup panko breadcrumbs

2⅓ cups cooked brown Jasmine rice

2 green onions, chopped

¾ cup sweet onion dressing

DIRECTIONS

1 Preheat the air fryer to 350 degrees.

2 In a medium bowl, mix the ground turkey with the onion, garlic, thyme, cinnamon, cayenne pepper, paprika, salt, pepper, red pepper flakes, and brown sugar. Add the whisked egg and stir in the breadcrumbs until the turkey starts to hold together.

3 Using a 1-ounce scoop, portion the turkey into meatballs. You should get about 28 meatballs.

4 Spray the air fryer basket with olive oil spray.

5 Place the meatballs into the air fryer basket and cook for 5 minutes, shake the basket, and cook another 2 to 4 minutes (or until the internal temperature of the meatballs reaches 165 degrees).

6 Remove the meatballs from the basket and repeat for the remaining meatballs.

7 Serve warm over a bed of rice with chopped green onions and spicy Caribbean jerk dressing.

NOTE: Store any leftover meatballs in an airtight container in the refrigerator for up to 7 days or freeze for up to 3 months.

NOTE: If you prefer a slider type of meal, serve meatballs on Hawaiian rolls.

TIP: You can purchase a premade jerk seasoning and dressing in the spice and condiment section of many markets. Use 1 tablespoon of jerk seasoning in place of the spices.

VARY IT! Use a different spice blend if you like (see Chapter 2).

Southwest Gluten-Free Turkey Meatloaf

PREP TIME: 10 MIN	COOK TIME: 35 MIN	YIELD: 8 SERVINGS

INGREDIENTS

1 pound lean ground turkey

¼ cup corn grits

¼ cup diced onion

1 teaspoon minced garlic

½ teaspoon black pepper

½ teaspoon salt

1 large egg

½ cup ketchup

4 teaspoons chipotle hot sauce

⅓ cup shredded cheddar cheese

DIRECTIONS

1 Preheat the air fryer to 350 degrees.

2 In a large bowl, mix together the ground turkey, corn grits, onion, garlic, black pepper, and salt.

3 In a small bowl, whisk the egg. Add the egg to the turkey mixture and combine.

4 In a small bowl, mix the ketchup and hot sauce. Set aside.

5 Liberally spray a 9-x-4-inch loaf pan with olive oil spray. Depending on the size of your air fryer, you may need to use 2 or 3 mini loaf pans.

6 Spoon the ground turkey mixture into the loaf pan and evenly top with half of the ketchup mixture. Cover with foil and place the meatloaf into the air fryer. Cook for 30 minutes; remove the foil and discard. Check the internal temperature (it should be nearing 165 degrees).

7 Coat the top of the meatloaf with the remaining ketchup mixture, and sprinkle the cheese over the top. Place the meatloaf back in the air fryer for the remaining 5 minutes (or until the internal temperature reaches 165 degrees).

8 Remove from the oven and let cool 5 minutes before serving. Serve warm with desired sides.

NOTE: If you're using smaller loaf pans, you may need to decrease the total cook time to 30 minutes. Check the internal temperature at 25 minutes and then cook until it reaches doneness of 165 degrees.

TIP: Serve with black beans and fresh guacamole.

VARY IT! Don't have corn grits? Swap in a cooked brown rice to keep this gluten free or 1/3 cup of breadcrumbs.

Stuffed Pork Chops

PREP TIME: 15 MIN	COOK TIME: 12 MIN	YIELD: 4 SERVINGS

INGREDIENTS

4 boneless pork chops

½ teaspoon salt

½ teaspoon black pepper

¼ teaspoon paprika

1 cup frozen spinach, defrosted and squeezed dry

2 cloves garlic, minced

2 ounces cream cheese

¼ cup grated Parmesan cheese

1 tablespoon extra-virgin olive oil

DIRECTIONS

1 Pat the pork chops with a paper towel. Make a slit in the side of each pork chop to create a pouch.

2 Season the pork chops with the salt, pepper, and paprika.

3 In a small bowl, mix together the spinach, garlic, cream cheese, and Parmesan cheese.

4 Divide the mixture into fourths and stuff the pork chop pouches. Secure the pouches with toothpicks.

5 Preheat the air fryer to 400 degrees.

6 Place the stuffed pork chops in the air fryer basket and spray liberally with cooking spray. Cook for 6 minutes, flip and coat with more cooking spray, and cook another 6 minutes. Check to make sure the meat is cooked to an internal temperature of 145 degrees. Cook the pork chops in batches, as needed.

TIP: Serve with roasted potatoes and sautéed carrots to complete the meal.

VARY IT! Try a cornbread stuffing or prosciutto and cheese instead.

Pork Schnitzel

PREP TIME: 15 MIN	COOK TIME: 14 MIN	YIELD: 4 SERVINGS

INGREDIENTS

4 boneless pork chops, pounded to ¼-inch thickness

1 teaspoon salt, divided

1 teaspoon black pepper, divided

½ cup all-purpose flour

2 eggs

1 cup breadcrumbs

¼ teaspoon paprika

1 lemon, cut into wedges

DIRECTIONS

1 Season both sides of the pork chops with ½ teaspoon of the salt and ½ teaspoon of the pepper.

2 On a plate, place the flour.

3 In a large bowl, whisk the eggs.

4 In another large bowl, place the breadcrumbs.

5 Season the flour with the paprika and season the breadcrumbs with the remaining ½ teaspoon of salt and ½ teaspoon of pepper.

6 To bread the pork, place a pork chop in the flour, then into the whisked eggs, and then into the breadcrumbs. Place the breaded pork onto a plate and finish breading the remaining pork chops.

7 Preheat the air fryer to 390 degrees.

8 Place the pork chops into the air fryer, not overlapping and working in batches as needed. Spray the pork chops with cooking spray and cook for 8 minutes; flip the pork and cook for another 4 to 6 minutes or until cooked to an internal temperature of 145 degrees.

9 Serve with lemon wedges.

TIP: Serve with spätzle and a tossed salad to complete this German meal.

Chapter 12

Seafood Mains

I f you haven't heard the news, seafood is *very* good for your health — so much so that most nutrition organizations recommend consuming it at least twice a week as part of a healthy diet.

To get you onboard the seafood ship, we've re-created some fan favorite traditional fare you'd find while dining out. But all these recipes are a bit healthier because they're air fried, not deep fried! You'd be surprised how much flavor is there when you have the right seasonings to really make these seafood dishes come to life.

Liz's family is keen on Tuna Patties with Dill Sauce, but Wendy Jo's is all for the Maple-Crusted Salmon. You may find out for yourself that your family has a preference for a certain type of fish. Putting that recipe on repeat in your rotation until you're ready to branch out and try something new is perfectly okay!

Bottom line: Eat more seafood, and let this chapter be your guide!

Calamari Fritti

PREP TIME: 40 MIN	COOK TIME: 8 MIN	YIELD: 4 SERVINGS

INGREDIENTS

1 pound calamari, cleaned and sliced into rings

¼ cup lemon juice

¼ cup cornstarch

2 eggs

¼ cup all-purpose flour

1 teaspoon salt, divided

¼ cup semolina flour or cornmeal

¼ teaspoon paprika

2 medium tomatoes, diced

2 cloves garlic, chopped

4 basil leaves, thinly sliced

1 lemon, cut into 8 wedges for serving

DIRECTIONS

1 In a medium bowl, mix together the calamari rings and lemon juice; set aside to marinate for 10 minutes. Drain and pat the calamari with paper towel to slightly dry.

2 Preheat the air fryer to 360 degrees F.

3 In a small bowl, place the cornstarch.

4 In a second bowl, whisk the eggs.

5 In a third bowl, add the flour, ½ teaspoon of the salt, the semolina flour, and the paprika.

6 Working in small batches, dredge the calamari rings first in the cornstarch; shake off the excess. Then dip the rings into the beaten eggs and then into the flour mixture; shake off the excess. Place the rings in the air fryer basket, making sure the rings don't touch each other, and spray liberally with cooking spray. Cook for 4 minutes, toss the rings, and continue cooking another 4 minutes, until golden brown.

7 Meanwhile, in a medium bowl, mix together the tomatoes, garlic, basil, and the remaining ½ teaspoon of salt.

8 To serve, sprinkle the calamari with the tomato mixture and serve with lemon wedges.

NOTE: Semolina flour is durum wheat, but the texture of semolina is closer to a finely ground cornmeal.

TIP: Don't overcook calamari! Soaking in lemon juice prior to cooking helps tenderize and slightly cook the calamari. When the calamari gets lightly browned, check for doneness. If the calamari are chewy, they've been overcooked.

VARY IT! Serve with a Sriracha mayonnaise for a fun twist on this traditional Mediterranean dish.

Crab Cakes

PREP TIME: 10 MIN | COOK TIME: 9 MIN | YIELD: 4 SERVINGS

INGREDIENTS

1 pound lump crab meat, checked for shells

⅓ cup breadcrumbs

¼ cup finely chopped onions

¼ cup finely chopped red bell peppers

¼ cup finely chopped parsley

¼ teaspoon sea salt

2 eggs, whisked

¾ cup mayonnaise, divided

¼ cup sour cream

1 lemon, divided

¼ cup sweet pickle relish

1 tablespoon prepared mustard

DIRECTIONS

1 In a large bowl, mix together the crab meat, breadcrumbs, onions, bell peppers, parsley, sea salt, eggs, and ¼ cup of the mayonnaise.

2 Preheat the air fryer to 380 degrees.

3 Form 8 patties with the crab cake mixture. Line the air fryer basket with parchment paper and place the crab cakes on the parchment paper. Spray with cooking spray. Cook for 4 minutes, turn over the crab cakes, spray with cooking spray, and cook for an additional 3 to 5 minutes, or until golden brown and the edges are crispy. Cook in batches as needed.

4 Meanwhile, make the sauce. In a small bowl, mix together the remaining ½ cup of mayonnaise, the sour cream, the juice from ½ of the lemon, the pickle relish, and the mustard.

5 Place the cooked crab cakes on a serving platter and serve with the remaining ½ lemon cut into wedges and the dipping sauce.

NOTE: When using a thermometer to test for doneness, the crab cakes should reach 155 degrees.

NOTE: Crab meat can be slightly salty, so adjust the seasoning after cooking as needed.

TIP: Serve the crab cakes on a bed of greens for a complete meal.

VARY IT! Crab cakes can be made with a variety of flavors and fillers. If your preference is gluten-free, opt for crushed gluten-free crackers in place of the breadcrumbs.

Tuna Patties with Dill Sauce

PREP TIME: 40 MIN | COOK TIME: 10 MIN | YIELD: 6 SERVINGS

INGREDIENTS

Two 5-ounce cans albacore tuna, drained

½ teaspoon garlic powder

2 teaspoons dried dill, divided

½ teaspoon black pepper

½ teaspoon salt, divided

¼ cup minced onion

1 large egg

7 tablespoons mayonnaise, divided

¼ cup panko breadcrumbs

1 teaspoon fresh lemon juice

¼ teaspoon fresh lemon zest

6 pieces butterleaf lettuce

1 cup diced tomatoes

DIRECTIONS

1 In a large bowl, mix the tuna with the garlic powder, 1 teaspoon of the dried dill, the black pepper, ¼ teaspoon of the salt, and the onion. Make sure to use the back of a fork to really break up the tuna so there are no large chunks.

2 Mix in the egg and 1 tablespoon of the mayonnaise; then fold in the breadcrumbs so the tuna begins to form a thick batter that holds together.

3 Portion the tuna mixture into 6 equal patties and place on a plate lined with parchment paper in the refrigerator for at least 30 minutes. This will help the patties hold together in the air fryer.

4 When ready to cook, preheat the air fryer to 350 degrees.

5 Liberally spray the metal trivet that sits inside the air fryer basket with olive oil mist and place the patties onto the trivet.

6 Cook for 5 minutes, flip, and cook another 5 minutes.

7 While the patties are cooking, make the dill sauce by combining the remaining 6 tablespoons of mayonnaise with the remaining 1 teaspoon of dill, the lemon juice, the lemon zest, and the remaining ¼ teaspoon of salt. Set aside.

8 Remove the patties from the air fryer.

9 Place 1 slice of lettuce on a plate and top with the tuna patty and a tomato slice. Repeat to form the remaining servings. Drizzle the dill dressing over the top. Serve immediately.

NOTE: The tuna patties will keep in an airtight container for up to 5 days in the refrigerator or 3 months in the freezer. Store the sauce in a locked jar in the refrigerator and use within 10 days.

NOTE: If you don't have a metal trivet, you can place the patties directly into the air fryer basket. Just be sure to liberally spray the basket with olive oil and watch them closely so they don't burn.

Bacon-Wrapped Scallops

PREP TIME: 10 MIN	COOK TIME: 8 MIN	YIELD: 4 SERVINGS

INGREDIENTS

16 large scallops

8 bacon strips

½ teaspoon black pepper

¼ teaspoon smoked paprika

DIRECTIONS

1 Pat the scallops dry with a paper towel. Slice each of the bacon strips in half. Wrap 1 bacon strip around 1 scallop and secure with a toothpick. Repeat with the remaining scallops. Season the scallops with pepper and paprika.

2 Preheat the air fryer to 350 degrees.

3 Place the bacon-wrapped scallops in the air fryer basket and cook for 4 minutes, shake the basket, cook another 3 minutes, shake the basket, and cook another 1 to 3 to minutes. When the bacon is crispy, the scallops should be cooked through and slightly firm, but not rubbery. Serve immediately.

NOTE: Scallops should be cooked to an internal temperature of 145 degrees.

NOTE: If your scallops are cooking much faster than the bacon, precook the bacon for 3 minutes at 400 degrees first; then wrap the scallops.

TIP: Serve as an appetizer or plate them on a bed of greens for a savory salad meal.

VARY IT! For a Mediterranean twist, wrap the scallops in prosciutto instead of bacon. For a plant-forward meal, wrap in roasted red bell peppers.

Firecracker Popcorn Shrimp

PREP TIME: 15 MIN	COOK TIME: 8 MIN	YIELD: 6 SERVINGS

INGREDIENTS

½ cup all-purpose flour

2 teaspoons ground paprika

1 teaspoon garlic powder

½ teaspoon black pepper

¼ teaspoon salt

2 eggs, whisked

1½ cups panko breadcrumbs

1 pound small shrimp, peeled and deveined

DIRECTIONS

1 Preheat the air fryer to 360 degrees.

2 In a medium bowl, place the flour and mix in the paprika, garlic powder, pepper, and salt.

3 In a shallow dish, place the eggs.

4 In a third dish, place the breadcrumbs.

5 Assemble the shrimp by covering them in the flour, then dipping them into the egg, and then coating them with the breadcrumbs. Repeat until all the shrimp are covered in the breading.

6 Liberally spray the metal trivet that fits in the air fryer basket with olive oil mist. Place the shrimp onto the trivet, leaving space between the shrimp to flip. Cook for 4 minutes, flip the shrimp, and cook another 4 minutes. Repeat until all the shrimp are cooked.

7 Serve warm with desired dipping sauce.

NOTE: You can cook the shrimp straight in the basket if you don't have a metal trivet. Just make sure to spray the basket with olive oil and watch carefully to prevent overcooking the shrimp.

NOTE: The internal temperature of the shrimp should be 145 degrees when cooked through.

VARY IT! Prefer a less spicy shrimp? Skip the paprika.

Coconut Shrimp

PREP TIME: 10 MIN	COOK TIME: 15 MIN	YIELD: 4 SERVINGS

INGREDIENTS

¼ cup cassava flour

1 teaspoon sugar

¼ teaspoon black pepper

½ teaspoon salt

2 large eggs

1 cup shredded coconut flakes, unsweetened

½ pound deveined, tail-off large shrimp

DIRECTIONS

1 Preheat the air fryer to 330 degrees. Spray the fryer basket with olive oil spray. Set aside.

2 In a small bowl, mix the flour, sugar, pepper, and salt.

3 In a separate bowl, whisk the eggs.

4 In a third bowl, place the coconut flakes.

5 Place 1 shrimp at a time in the flour mixture, then wash with the eggs, and cover with coconut flakes.

6 Liberally spray the metal trivet that fits inside the air fryer basket with olive oil spray. Place the shrimp onto the metal trivet and cook for 15 minutes, flipping halfway through. Repeat until all shrimp are cooked.

7 Serve immediately with desired sauce.

NOTE: You can cook the shrimp straight in the basket if you don't have a metal trivet. Just make sure to spray the basket olive oil and watch carefully to prevent overcooking the shrimp.

NOTE: If you can't find unsweetened coconut flakes, omit the sugar in the flour mixture and use sweetened coconut flakes instead.

TIP: Feel free to use whatever size shrimp you prefer. It's easier if they're already deveined with the tail off, just to save you time!

Shrimp Po'boy with Remoulade Sauce

PREP TIME: 15 MIN | **COOK TIME: 8 MIN** | **YIELD: 6 SERVINGS**

INGREDIENTS

½ cup all-purpose flour

½ teaspoon paprika

1 teaspoon garlic powder

½ teaspoon black pepper

¼ teaspoon salt

2 eggs, whisked

1½ cups panko breadcrumbs

1 pound small shrimp, peeled and deveined

Six 6-inch French rolls

2 cups shredded lettuce

12 ⅛-inch tomato slices

¾ cup Remoulade Sauce (see the following recipe)

DIRECTIONS

1 Preheat the air fryer to 360 degrees.

2 In a medium bowl, mix the flour, paprika, garlic powder, pepper, and salt.

3 In a shallow dish, place the eggs.

4 In a third dish, place the panko breadcrumbs.

5 Covering the shrimp in the flour, dip them into the egg, and coat them with the breadcrumbs. Repeat until all shrimp are covered in the breading.

6 Liberally spray the metal trivet that fits inside the air fryer basket with olive oil spray. Place the shrimp onto the trivet, leaving space between the shrimp to flip. Cook for 4 minutes, flip the shrimp, and cook another 4 minutes. Repeat until all the shrimp are cooked.

7 Slice the rolls in half. Stuff each roll with shredded lettuce, tomato slices, breaded shrimp, and remoulade sauce. Serve immediately.

NOTE: You can cook the shrimp straight in the basket if you don't have a metal trivet. Just make sure to spray the basket olive oil and watch carefully to prevent overcooking the shrimp.

NOTE: Store the shrimp in an airtight container in the refrigerator for up to 3 days. Reheat in the air fryer at 350 degrees for 3 to 5 minutes before serving.

TIP: You can go for store-bought remoulade sauce if you're short on time.

Remoulade Sauce

INGREDIENTS

¾ cup mayonnaise

1 teaspoon mustard

1 teaspoon hot sauce

1 teaspoon minced garlic

½ teaspoon Cajun seasoning

½ teaspoon black pepper

¼ teaspoon salt

1 tablespoon relish

1 tablespoon fresh lemon juice

DIRECTIONS

Place all the ingredients in a bowl and whisk until smooth.

NOTE: Store in an airtight container in the refrigerator for up to 10 days.

Honey Pecan Shrimp

PREP TIME: 15 MIN	COOK TIME: 10 MIN	YIELD: 4 SERVINGS

INGREDIENTS

¼ cup cornstarch

¾ teaspoon sea salt, divided

¼ teaspoon pepper

2 egg whites

⅔ cup finely chopped pecans

1 pound raw, peeled, and deveined shrimp

¼ cup honey

2 tablespoons mayonnaise

DIRECTIONS

1   In a small bowl, whisk together the cornstarch, ½ teaspoon of the salt, and the pepper.

2   In a second bowl, whisk together the egg whites until soft and foamy. (They don't need to be whipped to peaks or even soft peaks, just frothy.)

3   In a third bowl, mix together the pecans and the remaining ¼ teaspoon of sea salt.

4   Pat the shrimp dry with paper towels. Working in small batches, dip the shrimp into the cornstarch, then into the egg whites, and then into the pecans until all the shrimp are coated with pecans.

5   Preheat the air fryer to 330 degrees.

6   Place the coated shrimp inside the air fryer basket and spray with cooking spray. Cook for 5 minutes, toss the shrimp, and cook another 5 minutes.

7   Meanwhile, place the honey in a microwave-safe bowl and microwave for 30 seconds. Whisk in the mayonnaise until smooth and creamy. Pour the honey sauce into a serving bowl. Add the cooked shrimp to the serving bowl while hot and toss to coat. Serve immediately.

NOTE: Shrimp are cooked when they're pink and firm. Overcooking shrimp will result in a rubbery texture. If using a thermometer, check for 145 degrees.

TIP: Serve with steamed rice and steamed broccoli to complete the meal.

VARY IT! Walnuts, pistachios, or sesame seeds can all be used in place of the pecans.

Blackened Catfish

PREP TIME: 5 MIN	COOK TIME: 8 MIN	YIELD: 4 SERVINGS

INGREDIENTS

1 teaspoon paprika

1 teaspoon garlic powder

1 teaspoon onion powder

1 teaspoon ground dried thyme

½ teaspoon ground black pepper

⅛ teaspoon cayenne pepper

½ teaspoon dried oregano

⅛ teaspoon crushed red pepper flakes

1 pound catfish filets

½ teaspoon sea salt

2 tablespoons butter, melted

1 tablespoon extra-virgin olive oil

2 tablespoons chopped parsley

1 lemon, cut into wedges

DIRECTIONS

1 In a small bowl, stir together the paprika, garlic powder, onion powder, thyme, black pepper, cayenne pepper, oregano, and crushed red pepper flakes.

2 Pat the fish dry with paper towels. Season the filets with sea salt and then coat with the blackening seasoning.

3 In a small bowl, mix together the butter and olive oil and drizzle over the fish filets, flipping them to coat them fully.

4 Preheat the air fryer to 350 degrees.

5 Place the fish in the air fryer basket and cook for 8 minutes, checking the fish for doneness after 4 minutes. The fish will flake easily when cooked.

6 Remove the fish from the air fryer. Top with chopped parsley and serve with lemon wedges.

NOTE: If you prefer a less spicy dish, omit the cayenne pepper and crushed red pepper flakes.

TIP: Serve blackened catfish with mashed potatoes and steamed green beans to complete the meal.

VARY IT! If you can't find catfish, try any firm white fish in its place.

Pecan-Crusted Tilapia

PREP TIME: 5 MIN	COOK TIME: 8 MIN	YIELD: 4 SERVINGS

INGREDIENTS

1 pound skinless, boneless tilapia filets

¼ cup butter, melted

1 teaspoon minced fresh or dried rosemary

1 cup finely chopped pecans

1 teaspoon sea salt

¼ teaspoon paprika

2 tablespoons chopped parsley

1 lemon, cut into wedges

DIRECTIONS

1 Pat the tilapia filets dry with paper towels.

2 Pour the melted butter over the filets and flip the filets to coat them completely.

3 In a medium bowl, mix together the rosemary, pecans, salt, and paprika.

4 Preheat the air fryer to 350 degrees.

5 Place the tilapia filets into the air fryer basket and top with the pecan coating. Cook for 6 to 8 minutes. The fish should be firm to the touch and flake easily when fully cooked.

6 Remove the fish from the air fryer. Top the fish with chopped parsley and serve with lemon wedges.

TIP: Serve with steamed rice and cabbage slaw to complete the meal.

VARY IT! Any firm white fish can be used in place of tilapia.

Maple-Crusted Salmon

PREP TIME: 35 MIN | COOK TIME: 8 MIN | YIELD: 2 SERVINGS

INGREDIENTS

12 ounces salmon filets

⅓ cup maple syrup

1 teaspoon Worcestershire sauce

2 teaspoons Dijon mustard or brown mustard

½ cup finely chopped walnuts

½ teaspoon sea salt

½ lemon

1 tablespoon chopped parsley, for garnish

DIRECTIONS

1 Place the salmon in a shallow baking dish. Top with maple syrup, Worcestershire sauce, and mustard. Refrigerate for 30 minutes.

2 Preheat the air fryer to 350 degrees.

3 Remove the salmon from the marinade and discard the marinade.

4 Place the chopped nuts on top of the salmon filets, and sprinkle salt on top of the nuts. Place the salmon, skin side down, in the air fryer basket. Cook for 6 to 8 minutes or until the fish flakes in the center.

5 Remove the salmon and plate on a serving platter. Squeeze fresh lemon over the top of the salmon and top with chopped parsley. Serve immediately.

NOTE: If using a thermometer, the internal temperature of cooked salmon should read 145 degrees. Thicker pieces of salmon will take longer to cook; be sure to check for doneness.

TIP: Serve salmon with steamed broccoli and roasted potatoes.

VARY IT! When swapping out toppings, consider a fattier nut or seed to avoid burning. Sesame seeds are a great nut-free topping.

Garlic and Dill Salmon

PREP TIME: 5 MIN | COOK TIME: 8 MIN | YIELD: 2 SERVINGS

INGREDIENTS

12 ounces salmon filets with skin

2 tablespoons melted butter

1 tablespoon extra-virgin olive oil

2 garlic cloves, minced

1 tablespoon fresh dill

½ teaspoon sea salt

½ lemon

DIRECTIONS

1 Pat the salmon dry with paper towels.

2 In a small bowl, mix together the melted butter, olive oil, garlic, and dill.

3 Sprinkle the top of the salmon with sea salt. Brush all sides of the salmon with the garlic and dill butter.

4 Preheat the air fryer to 350 degrees.

5 Place the salmon, skin side down, in the air fryer basket. Cook for 6 to 8 minutes, or until the fish flakes in the center.

6 Remove the salmon and plate on a serving platter. Squeeze fresh lemon over the top of the salmon. Serve immediately.

NOTE: The internal temperature of cooked salmon should read 145 degrees.

TIP: Serve with garlic buttered green beans, sliced tomatoes, and garlic bread to complete the meal.

VARY IT! Pair any of your favorite herbs or spices with the garlic. Our top picks are minced rosemary and garlic, cilantro lime and garlic, and basil and garlic.

Beer-Breaded Halibut Fish Tacos

PREP TIME: 35 MIN	COOK TIME: 10 MIN	YIELD: 4 SERVINGS

INGREDIENTS

1 pound halibut, cut into 1-inch strips

1 cup light beer

1 jalapeño, minced and divided

1 clove garlic, minced

¼ teaspoon ground cumin

½ cup cornmeal

¼ cup all-purpose flour

1¼ teaspoons sea salt, divided

2 cups shredded cabbage

1 lime, juiced and divided

¼ cup Greek yogurt

¼ cup mayonnaise

1 cup grape tomatoes, quartered

½ cup chopped cilantro

¼ cup chopped onion

1 egg, whisked

8 corn tortillas

DIRECTIONS

1 In a shallow baking dish, place the fish, the beer, 1 teaspoon of the minced jalapeño, the garlic, and the cumin. Cover and refrigerate for 30 minutes.

2 Meanwhile, in a medium bowl, mix together the cornmeal, flour, and ½ teaspoon of the salt.

3 In large bowl, mix together the shredded cabbage, 1 tablespoon of the lime juice, the Greek yogurt, the mayonnaise, and ½ teaspoon of the salt.

4 In a small bowl, make the pico de gallo by mixing together the tomatoes, cilantro, onion, ¼ teaspoon of the salt, the remaining jalapeño, and the remaining lime juice.

5 Remove the fish from the refrigerator and discard the marinade. Dredge the fish in the whisked egg; then dredge the fish in the cornmeal flour mixture, until all pieces of fish have been breaded.

6 Preheat the air fryer to 350 degrees.

7 Place the fish in the air fryer basket and spray liberally with cooking spray. Cook for 6 minutes, flip and shake the fish, and cook another 4 minutes.

8 While the fish is cooking, heat the tortillas in a heavy skillet for 1 to 2 minutes over high heat.

9 To assemble the tacos, place the battered fish on the heated tortillas, and top with slaw and pico de gallo. Serve immediately.

NOTE: Fresh corn tortillas will be more pliable and less stiff. You can use flour tortillas if you prefer.

NOTE: If you don't have cornmeal, you can use polenta or semolina flour instead.

Lightened-Up Breaded Fish Filets

PREP TIME: 15 MIN	COOK TIME: 10 MIN	YIELD: 4 SERVINGS

INGREDIENTS

½ cup all-purpose flour

½ teaspoon cayenne pepper

1 teaspoon garlic powder

½ teaspoon black pepper

¼ teaspoon salt

2 eggs, whisked

1½ cups panko breadcrumbs

1 pound boneless white fish filets

1 cup tartar sauce

1 lemon, sliced into wedges

DIRECTIONS

1 In a medium bowl, mix the flour, cayenne pepper, garlic powder, pepper, and salt.

2 In a shallow dish, place the eggs.

3 In a third dish, place the breadcrumbs.

4 Cover the fish in the flour, dip them in the egg, and coat them with panko. Repeat until all fish are covered in the breading.

5 Liberally spray the metal trivet that fits inside the air fryer basket with olive oil mist. Place the fish onto the trivet, leaving space between the filets to flip. Cook for 5 minutes, flip the fish, and cook another 5 minutes. Repeat until all the fish is cooked.

6 Serve warm with tartar sauce and lemon wedges.

NOTE: You can cook the fish straight in the basket if you don't have a metal trivet. Just make sure to spray the basket with olive oil and watch carefully to prevent burning.

NOTE: Store the fish in an airtight container in the refrigerator and use within 3 days. Reheat in the air fryer at 350 degrees for 5 minutes.

TIP: Tilapia and red snapper work well in this recipe. You can typically find both frozen and fresh at most major markets.

Chapter **13**

Vegetarian Mains

E ating plant forward is very trendy these days and for good reason: Produce is powerful! From fighting off disease to improving digestion, the benefits of incorporating more plant-based meals into your regular routine are profound. Whether you're vegetarian, vegan, or an omnivore, this chapter shows you how to make plant-forward main dishes without sacrificing any flavor. You can pair a simple Basic Fried Tofu with Veggie Fried Rice, or enjoy Charred Cauliflower Tacos on Taco Tuesday.

Prefer more of a traditional menu? Eggplant Parmesan may be right up your ally.

Have a little one at home? Lentil Fritters are the perfect first-bites meal that the whole family can enjoy.

We promise, with the recipes in this chapter, everyone will be pleased with incorporating more plant-based meals into your household menu!

Basic Fried Tofu

PREP TIME: 1 HR 20 MIN	COOK TIME: 17 MIN	YIELD: 4 SERVINGS

INGREDIENTS

14 ounces extra-firm tofu, drained and pressed

1 tablespoon sesame oil

2 tablespoons low-sodium soy sauce

¼ cup rice vinegar

1 tablespoon fresh grated ginger

1 clove garlic, minced

3 tablespoons cornstarch

¼ teaspoon black pepper

⅛ teaspoon salt

DIRECTIONS

1 Cut the tofu into 16 cubes. Set aside in a glass container with a lid.

2 In a medium bowl, mix the sesame oil, soy sauce, rice vinegar, ginger, and garlic. Pour over the tofu and secure the lid. Place in the refrigerator to marinate for an hour.

3 Preheat the air fryer to 350 degrees.

4 In a small bowl, mix the cornstarch, black pepper, and salt.

5 Transfer the tofu to a large bowl and discard the leftover marinade. Pour the cornstarch mixture over the tofu and toss until all the pieces are coated.

6 Liberally spray the air fryer basket with olive oil mist and set the tofu pieces inside. Allow space between the tofu so it can cook evenly. Cook in batches if necessary.

7 Cook 15 to 17 minutes, shaking the basket every 5 minutes to allow the tofu to cook evenly on all sides. When it's done cooking, the tofu will be crisped and browned on all sides.

8 Remove the tofu from the air fryer basket and serve warm.

NOTE: Press tofu before marinating by placing it between layers of paper towels under a heavy object (like a cast iron skillet). You can purchase a tofu press, but this homemade option works just as well.

NOTE: The tofu will keep in the refrigerator for 3 days in an airtight container. Reheat in the air fryer at 350 degrees for 3 to 5 minutes before serving.

TIP: Serve on top of a salad or bed of rice and steamed vegetables with desired dressing or sauce.

TIP: Want to make this gluten-free? Use a tamari or gluten-free soy sauce alternative

Veggie Fried Rice

PREP TIME: 30 MIN	COOK TIME: 25 MIN	YIELD: 4 SERVINGS

INGREDIENTS

1 cup cooked brown rice

⅓ cup chopped onion

½ cup chopped carrots

½ cup chopped bell peppers

½ cup chopped broccoli florets

3 tablespoons low-sodium soy sauce

1 tablespoon sesame oil

1 teaspoon ground ginger

1 teaspoon ground garlic powder

½ teaspoon black pepper

⅛ teaspoon salt

2 large eggs

DIRECTIONS

1 Preheat the air fryer to 370 degrees.

2 In a large bowl, mix together the brown rice, onions, carrots, bell pepper, and broccoli.

3 In a small bowl, whisk together the soy sauce, sesame oil, ginger, garlic powder, pepper, salt, and eggs.

4 Pour the egg mixture into the rice and vegetable mixture and mix together.

5 Liberally spray a 7-inch springform pan (or compatible air fryer dish) with olive oil. Add the rice mixture to the pan and cover with aluminum foil.

6 Place a metal trivet into the air fryer basket and set the pan on top. Cook for 15 minutes. Carefully remove the pan from basket, discard the foil, and mix the rice. Return the rice to the air fryer basket, turning down the temperature to 350 degrees and cooking another 10 minutes.

7 Remove and let cool 5 minutes. Serve warm.

NOTE: To keep this recipe gluten-free, use a tamari or other gluten-free soy sauce.

TIP: Serve with a fried egg over the top for an added vegetarian protein boost.

VARY IT! Prefer a little meat? Mix in a cup of cooked chicken, pork, or beef.

Spicy Sesame Tempeh Slaw with Peanut Dressing

PREP TIME: 2 HR 10 MIN	COOK TIME: 8 MIN	YIELD: 2 SERVINGS

INGREDIENTS

2 cups hot water

1 teaspoon salt

8 ounces tempeh, sliced into 1-inch-long pieces

2 tablespoons low-sodium soy sauce

2 tablespoons rice vinegar

1 tablespoon filtered water

2 teaspoons sesame oil

½ teaspoon fresh ginger

1 clove garlic, minced

¼ teaspoon black pepper

½ jalapeño, sliced

4 cups cabbage slaw

4 tablespoons Peanut Dressing (see the following recipe)

2 tablespoons fresh chopped cilantro

2 tablespoons chopped peanuts

DIRECTIONS

1 Mix the hot water with the salt and pour over the tempeh in a glass bowl. Stir and cover with a towel for 10 minutes.

2 Discard the water and leave the tempeh in the bowl.

3 In a medium bowl, mix the soy sauce, rice vinegar, filtered water, sesame oil, ginger, garlic, pepper, and jalapeño. Pour over the tempeh and cover with a towel. Place in the refrigerator to marinate for at least 2 hours.

4 Preheat the air fryer to 370 degrees. Remove the tempeh from the bowl and discard the remaining marinade.

5 Liberally spray the metal trivet that goes into the air fryer basket and place the tempeh on top of the trivet.

6 Cook for 4 minutes, flip, and cook another 4 minutes.

7 In a large bowl, mix the cabbage slaw with the Peanut Dressing and toss in the cilantro and chopped peanuts.

8 Portion onto 4 plates and place the cooked tempeh on top when cooking completes. Serve immediately.

NOTE: Prep a day ahead for a stronger flavor infusion.

Peanut Dressing

PREP TIME: 5 MIN	COOK TIME: NONE	YIELD: 10 SERVINGS

INGREDIENTS

½ cup creamy peanut butter

½ lime, juiced

2 tablespoons rice vinegar

1 tablespoon cane sugar

2 tablespoons low-sodium soy sauce or tamari

1 teaspoon fresh ground ginger

¼ cup water

1 teaspoon Sriracha

1 tablespoon sesame oil

1 garlic clove, minced

DIRECTIONS

1 Using a fork, whisk together all ingredients in a medium bowl. Add more water if you prefer a thinner dressing. You can also use a blender to mix the ingredients.

2 Serve immediately or store in an airtight container in the refrigerator for up to 10 days.

Charred Cauliflower Tacos

PREP TIME: 15 MIN	COOK TIME: 10 MIN	YIELD: 4 SERVINGS

INGREDIENTS

1 head cauliflower, washed and cut into florets

2 tablespoons avocado oil

2 teaspoons taco seasoning

1 medium avocado

½ teaspoon garlic powder

¼ teaspoon black pepper

¼ teaspoon salt

2 tablespoons chopped red onion

2 teaspoons fresh squeezed lime juice

¼ cup chopped cilantro

Eight 6-inch corn tortillas

½ cup cooked corn

½ cup shredded purple cabbage

DIRECTIONS

1 Preheat the air fryer to 390 degrees.

2 In a large bowl, toss the cauliflower with the avocado oil and taco seasoning. Set the metal trivet inside the air fryer basket and liberally spray with olive oil.

3 Place the cauliflower onto the trivet and cook for 10 minutes, shaking every 3 minutes to allow for an even char.

4 While the cauliflower is cooking, prepare the avocado sauce. In a medium bowl, mash the avocado; then mix in the garlic powder, pepper, salt, and onion. Stir in the lime juice and cilantro; set aside.

5 Remove the cauliflower from the air fryer basket.

6 Place 1 tablespoon of avocado sauce in the middle of a tortilla, and top with corn, cabbage, and charred cauliflower. Repeat with the remaining tortillas. Serve immediately.

NOTE: If you don't have a metal trivet, you can cook the cauliflower directly in the metal basket. Just be sure to shake the cauliflower frequently so it doesn't burn.

NOTE: Store the leftover cauliflower in an airtight container and use within 3 days. Reheat in the air fryer for 3 to 5 minutes at 350 degrees.

Cheesy Enchilada Stuffed Baked Potatoes

PREP TIME: 10 MIN	COOK TIME: 37 MIN	YIELD: 4 SERVINGS

INGREDIENTS

2 medium russet potatoes, washed

One 15-ounce can mild red enchilada sauce

One 15-ounce can low-sodium black beans, rinsed and drained

1 teaspoon taco seasoning

½ cup shredded cheddar cheese

1 medium avocado, halved

½ teaspoon garlic powder

¼ teaspoon black pepper

¼ teaspoon salt

2 teaspoons fresh lime juice

2 tablespoon chopped red onion

¼ cup chopped cilantro

DIRECTIONS

1. Preheat the air fryer to 390 degrees.

2. Puncture the outer surface of the potatoes with a fork.

3. Set the potatoes inside the air fryer basket and cook for 20 minutes, rotate, and cook another 10 minutes.

4. In a large bowl, mix the enchilada sauce, black beans, and taco seasoning.

5. When the potatoes have finished cooking, carefully remove them from the air fryer basket and let cool for 5 minutes.

6. Using a pair of tongs to hold the potato if it's still too hot to touch, slice the potato in half lengthwise. Use a spoon to scoop out the potato flesh and add it into the bowl with the enchilada sauce. Mash the potatoes with the enchilada sauce mixture, creating a uniform stuffing.

7. Place the potato skins into an air-fryer-safe pan and stuff the halves with the enchilada stuffing. Sprinkle the cheese over the top of each potato.

8. Set the air fryer temperature to 350 degrees, return the pan to the air fryer basket, and cook for another 5 to 7 minutes to heat the potatoes and melt the cheese.

9. While the potatoes are cooking, take the avocado and scoop out the flesh into a small bowl. Mash it with the back of a fork; then mix in the garlic powder, pepper, salt, lime juice, and onion. Set aside.

10. When the potatoes have finished cooking, remove the pan from the air fryer and place the potato halves on a plate. Top with avocado mash and fresh cilantro. Serve immediately.

Black Bean Empanadas

PREP TIME: 35 MIN | COOK TIME: 8 MIN | YIELD: 12 SERVINGS

INGREDIENTS

1½ cups all-purpose flour

1 cup whole-wheat flour

1 teaspoon salt

½ cup cold unsalted butter

1 egg

½ cup milk

One 14.5-ounce can black beans, drained and rinsed

¼ cup chopped cilantro

1 cup shredded purple cabbage

1 cup shredded Monterey jack cheese

¼ cup salsa

DIRECTIONS

1 In a food processor, place the all-purpose flour, whole-wheat flour, salt, and butter into processor and process for 2 minutes, scraping down the sides of the food processor every 30 seconds. Add in the egg and blend for 30 seconds. Using the pulse button, add in the milk 1 tablespoon at a time, or until dough is moist enough to handle and be rolled into a ball. Let the dough rest at room temperature for 30 minutes.

2 Meanwhile, in a large bowl, mix together the black beans, cilantro, cabbage, Monterey Jack cheese, and salsa.

3 On a floured surface, cut the dough in half; then form a ball and cut each ball into 6 equal pieces, totaling 12 equal pieces. Work with one piece at a time, and cover the remaining dough with a towel.

4 Roll out a piece of dough into a 6-inch round, much like a tortilla, ¼ inch thick. Place 4 tablespoons of filling in the center of the round, and fold over to form a half-circle. Using a fork, crimp the edges together and pierce the top for air holes. Repeat with the remaining dough and filling.

5 Preheat the air fryer to 350 degrees.

6 Working in batches, place 3 to 4 empanadas in the air fryer basket and spray with cooking spray. Cook for 4 minutes, flip over the empanadas and spray with cooking spray, and cook another 4 minutes.

TIP: Serve with a simple sauce of Greek yogurt, lime juice, cumin, and hot sauce or make it a slaw by adding in purple cabbage to the sauce.

VARY IT! Sweet potatoes and black beans are magic together. If you have leftover sweet potatoes around, chop them up and add them to the filling.

VARY IT! Refried beans are an easy swap for black beans.

Thai Peanut Veggie Burgers

PREP TIME: 20 MIN | **COOK TIME: 14 MIN** | **YIELD: 6 SERVINGS**

INGREDIENTS

One 15.5-ounce can cannellini beans

1 teaspoon minced garlic

¼ cup chopped onion

1 Thai chili pepper, sliced

2 tablespoons natural peanut butter

½ teaspoon black pepper

½ teaspoon salt

⅓ cup all-purpose flour (optional)

½ cup cooked quinoa

1 large carrot, grated

1 cup shredded red cabbage

¼ cup peanut dressing

¼ cup chopped cilantro

6 Hawaiian rolls

6 butterleaf lettuce leaves

DIRECTIONS

1 Preheat the air fryer to 350 degrees.

2 To a blender or food processor fitted with a metal blade, add the beans, garlic, onion, chili pepper, peanut butter, pepper, and salt. Pulse for 5 to 10 seconds. Do not over process. The mixture should be coarse, not smooth.

3 Remove from the blender or food processor and spoon into a large bowl. Mix in the cooked quinoa and carrots. At this point, the mixture should begin to hold together to form small patties. If the dough appears to be too sticky (meaning you likely processed a little too long), add the flour to hold the patties together.

4 Using a large spoon, form 8 equal patties out of the batter.

5 Liberally spray a metal trivet with olive oil spray and set in the air fryer basket. Place the patties into the basket, leaving enough space to be able to turn them with a spatula.

6 Cook for 7 minutes, flip, and cook another 7 minutes.

7 Remove from the heat and repeat with additional patties.

8 To serve, place the red cabbage in a bowl and toss with peanut dressing and cilantro. Place the veggie burger on a bun, and top with a slice of lettuce and cabbage slaw.

NOTE: If you don't have a metal trivet, you can place the burgers directly in the basket. Just be sure to liberally spray with olive oil mist so they don't stick.

NOTE: Store in an airtight container for up to 5 days in the refrigerator or up to 3 months in the freezer. Reheat in the air fryer at 350 degrees for 2 minutes per side.

TIP: Use the Peanut Dressing from the Spicy Sesame Tempeh Slaw earlier in this chapter for a homemade sauce.

TIP: Looking for a lower-carb option? Serve over an extra portion or two of cabbage slaw and skip the bun.

Lentil Fritters

PREP TIME: 10 MIN	COOK TIME: 12 MIN	YIELD: 9 SERVINGS

INGREDIENTS

1 cup cooked red lentils

1 cup riced cauliflower

½ medium zucchini, shredded (about 1 cup)

¼ cup finely chopped onion

¼ teaspoon salt

¼ teaspoon black pepper

½ teaspoon garlic powder

¼ teaspoon paprika

1 large egg

⅓ cup quinoa flour

DIRECTIONS

1 Preheat the air fryer to 370 degrees.

2 In a large bowl, mix the lentils, cauliflower, zucchini, onion, salt, pepper, garlic powder, and paprika. Mix in the egg and flour until a thick dough forms.

3 Using a large spoon, form the dough into 9 large fritters.

4 Liberally spray the air fryer basket with olive oil. Place the fritters into the basket, leaving space around each fritter so you can flip them.

5 Cook for 6 minutes, flip, and cook another 6 minutes.

6 Remove from the air fryer and repeat with the remaining fritters. Serve warm with desired sauce and sides.

NOTE: If you don't have a metal trivet, you can cook these straight in the air fryer basket. Just be sure to liberally spray the basket with olive oil spray to prevent the fritters from sticking.

NOTE: If you don't have quinoa flour, almond flour or all-purpose flour will also work — it just won't be as nutritionally dense!

TIP: If the dough is too sticky, add 1 tablespoon of flour at a time to help create a thicker consistency that will hold together in the fryer.

TIP: These fritters pair perfectly with a yogurt-based sauce, like a cucumber dill or Sriracha ranch.

VARY IT! Have different veggies on hand? Feel free to swap those in. Riced broccoli pairs perfectly here, too!

Tandoori Paneer Naan Pizza

PREP TIME: 1 HR	COOK TIME: 10 MIN	YIELD: 4 SERVINGS

INGREDIENTS

6 tablespoons plain Greek yogurt, divided

1¼ teaspoons garam marsala, divided

½ teaspoon turmeric, divided

¼ teaspoon garlic powder

½ teaspoon paprika, divided

½ teaspoon black pepper, divided

3 ounces paneer, cut into small cubes

1 tablespoon extra-virgin olive oil

2 teaspoons minced garlic

4 cups baby spinach

2 tablespoons marinara sauce

¼ teaspoon salt

2 plain naan breads (approximately 6 inches in diameter)

½ cup shredded part-skim mozzarella cheese

DIRECTIONS

1 Preheat the air fryer to 350 degrees.

2 In a small bowl, mix 2 tablespoons of the yogurt, ½ teaspoon of the garam marsala, ¼ teaspoon of the turmeric, the garlic powder, ¼ teaspoon of the paprika, and ¼ teaspoon of the black pepper. Toss the paneer cubes in the mixture and let marinate for at least an hour.

3 Meanwhile, in a pan, heat the olive oil over medium heat. Add in the minced garlic and sauté for 1 minute. Stir in the spinach and begin to cook until it wilts. Add in the remaining 4 tablespoons of yogurt and the marinara sauce. Stir in the remaining ¾ teaspoon of garam masala, the remaining ¼ teaspoon of turmeric, the remaining ¼ teaspoon of paprika, the remaining ¼ teaspoon of black pepper, and the salt. Let simmer a minute or two, and then remove from the heat.

4 Equally divide the spinach mixture amongst the two naan breads. Place 1½ ounces of the marinated paneer on each naan.

5 Liberally spray the air fryer basket with olive oil mist.

6 Use a spatula to pick up one naan and place it in the air fryer basket.

7 Cook for 4 minutes, open the basket and sprinkle ¼ cup of mozzarella cheese on top, and cook another 4 minutes.

8 Remove from the air fryer and repeat with the remaining naan.

9 Serve warm.

NOTE: Naan will not keep well in the refrigerator, so prepare your desired quantity and enjoy immediately.

TIP: Serve with a garden salad tossed with a light olive oil and lemon juice dressing.

Roasted Vegetable Pita Pizza

PREP TIME: 10 MIN	COOK TIME: 20 MIN	YIELD: 4 SERVINGS

INGREDIENTS

1 medium red bell pepper, seeded and cut into quarters

1 teaspoon extra-virgin olive oil

⅛ teaspoon black pepper

⅛ teaspoon salt

Two 6-inch whole-grain pita breads

6 tablespoons pesto sauce

¼ small red onion, thinly sliced

½ cup shredded part-skim mozzarella cheese

DIRECTIONS

1 Preheat the air fryer to 400 degrees.

2 In a small bowl, toss the bell peppers with the olive oil, pepper, and salt.

3 Place the bell peppers in the air fryer and cook for 15 minutes, shaking every 5 minutes to prevent burning.

4 Remove the peppers and set aside. Turn the air fryer temperature down to 350 degrees.

5 Lay the pita bread on a flat surface. Cover each with half the pesto sauce; then top with even portions of the red bell peppers and onions. Sprinkle cheese over the top. Spray the air fryer basket with olive oil mist.

6 Carefully lift the pita bread into the air fryer basket with a spatula.

7 Cook for 5 to 8 minutes, or until the outer edges begin to brown and the cheese is melted.

8 Serve warm with desired sides.

NOTE: Best served immediately. Flatbread pitas do not hold up well when stored and reheated.

TIP: Tight on time? Use roasted red bell peppers from a jar and finely mince the onion and toss on top.

VARY IT! Prefer a more traditional pizza? Sub the pesto for a marinara sauce and top with tomatoes and cheese. You can add your favorite Italian meats here, too!

Falafel

PREP TIME: 10 MIN | COOK TIME: 10 MIN | YIELD: 4 SERVINGS

INGREDIENTS

One 14.5-ounce can garbanzo beans (chickpeas), drained and rinsed

1 clove garlic, chopped

1 cup chopped parsley

½ cup chopped dill

½ teaspoon ground cumin

½ teaspoon ground coriander

1 teaspoon salt

¼ cup sesame seeds

½ cup breadcrumbs

DIRECTIONS

1 Preheat the air fryer to 350 degrees.

2 Pat the garbanzo beans dry with a towel. In a food processor, place the beans, garlic, parsley, dill, cumin, coriander, and salt. Blend for 2 minutes, scraping down the sides of the food processor every 30 seconds.

3 In a small bowl, mix together the breadcrumbs and sesame seeds. Working one at a time and using a cookie scoop or approximately 2 tablespoons, form a patty about ½ inch thick and round. Dredge the patties in the breadcrumb mixture.

4 Place the falafel in the air fryer basket, making sure they don't overlap. Spray with cooking spray and cook for 6 minutes, flip over, and cook another 4 to 6 minutes. Cook in batches as needed.

TIP: Serve with the Cucumber Yogurt Sauce in Chapter 18.

TIP: These are great wrapped in a pita for a sandwich or served on a bed of greens for a salad.

VARY IT! Lentils or black beans make for a great bean patty. Feel free to swap out beans or herbs as desired.

Pizza Portobello Mushrooms

PREP TIME: 15 MIN	COOK TIME: 18 MIN	YIELD: 2 SERVINGS

INGREDIENTS

2 portobello mushroom caps, gills removed (see Figure 13-1)

1 teaspoon extra-virgin olive oil

¼ cup diced onion

1 teaspoon minced garlic

1 medium zucchini, shredded

1 teaspoon dried oregano

½ teaspoon black pepper

¼ teaspoon salt

⅓ cup marinara sauce

¼ cup shredded part-skim mozzarella cheese

¼ teaspoon red pepper flakes

2 tablespoons Parmesan cheese

2 tablespoons chopped basil

DIRECTIONS

1 Preheat the air fryer to 370 degrees.

2 Lightly spray the mushrooms with an olive oil mist and place into the air fryer to cook for 10 minutes, cap side up.

3 Add the olive oil to a pan and sauté the onion and garlic together for about 2 to 4 minutes. Stir in the zucchini, oregano, pepper, and salt, and continue to cook. When the zucchini has cooked down (usually about 4 to 6 minutes), add in the marinara sauce. Remove from the heat and stir in the mozzarella cheese.

4 Remove the mushrooms from the air fryer basket when cooking completes. Reset the temperature to 350 degrees.

5 Using a spoon, carefully stuff the mushrooms with the zucchini marinara mixture.

6 Return the stuffed mushrooms to the air fryer basket and cook for 5 to 8 minutes, or until the cheese is lightly browned. You should be able to easily insert a fork into the mushrooms when they're cooked.

7 Remove the mushrooms and sprinkle the red pepper flakes, Parmesan cheese, and fresh basil over the top.

8 Serve warm.

NOTE: Store any leftovers in an airtight container in the refrigerator and eat within 3 days. To reheat, preheat the air fryer to 350 degrees and cook for 5 minutes.

VARY IT! Prefer a heartier meal? Feel free to add in some cooked ground pork, beef, or lentils for a vegetarian option!

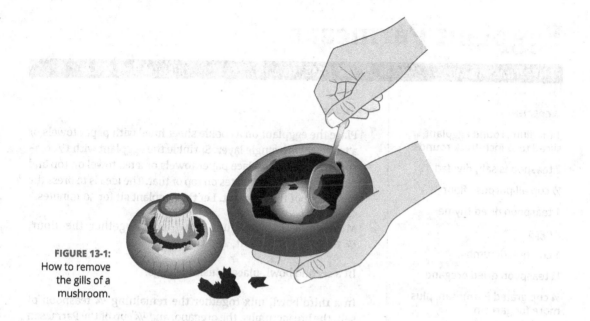

FIGURE 13-1:
How to remove
the gills of a
mushroom.

Eggplant Parmesan

PREP TIME: 40 MIN	COOK TIME: 10 MIN	YIELD: 4 SERVINGS

INGREDIENTS

1 medium, round eggplant, sliced to ½-inch-thick rounds

2 teaspoons salt, divided

½ cup all-purpose flour

1 teaspoon dried thyme

2 eggs

1 cup breadcrumbs

½ teaspoon dried oregano

¼ cup grated Parmesan, plus more for garnish

2 cups marinara sauce

2 tablespoons chopped parsley, for garnish

DIRECTIONS

1 Place the eggplant on a cookie sheet lined with paper towels or a tea towel in a single layer. Sprinkle the eggplant with 1½ teaspoons of the salt. Place paper towels or a tea towel on top and place heavier pots or plates on top of that. The idea is to press the bitters out of the eggplant. Let the eggplant sit for 30 minutes.

2 Meanwhile, in a medium bowl, mix together the flour, ¼ teaspoon of the salt, and the thyme.

3 In a second bowl, place whisk the eggs.

4 In a third bowl, mix together the remaining ¼ teaspoon of salt, the breadcrumbs, the oregano, and ¼ cup of the Parmesan cheese.

5 Preheat the air fryer to 370 degrees.

6 Remove the towels and rinse the eggplant slices. Pat the slices dry and begin breading the eggplant. Working with 1 slice at a time, first dip in the flour mixture; shake off the extra flour. Next, dip into the eggs. Finally, dredge the eggplant in the breading. Repeat with the remaining eggplant slices.

7 Place a single layer of eggplant slices in the air fryer basket and spray liberally with cooking spray. Cook for 5 minutes, flip over and spray with cooking spray, and cook another 5 minutes.

8 Meanwhile, heat the marinara sauce in a saucepan until warm.

9 To serve, plate the eggplant rounds and spoon the marinara over each round. Sprinkle with Parmesan cheese and parsley for garnish. Serve hot or at room temperature.

NOTE: Japanese eggplants are much thinner than American eggplant. Look for round and firm-skinned eggplant for best results.

TIP: Complete the meal with a green salad.

VARY IT! To serve as a baked casserole, layer air-fried eggplants with marinara and shredded mozzarella or fontina cheeses. Bake at 350 degrees for 25 minutes.

Arancini with Marinara

PREP TIME: 20 MIN	COOK TIME: 15 MIN	YIELD: 6 SERVINGS

INGREDIENTS

2 cups cooked rice

1 cup grated Parmesan cheese

1 egg, whisked

¼ teaspoon dried thyme

½ teaspoon dried oregano

½ teaspoon dried basil

½ teaspoon dried parsley

1 teaspoon salt

¼ teaspoon paprika

1 cup breadcrumbs

4 ounces mozzarella, cut into 24 cubes

2 cups marinara sauce

DIRECTIONS

1 In a large bowl, mix together the rice, Parmesan cheese, and egg.

2 In another bowl, mix together the thyme, oregano, basil, parsley, salt, paprika, and breadcrumbs.

3 Form 24 rice balls with the rice mixture. Use your thumb to make an indentation in the center and stuff 1 cube of mozzarella in the center of the rice; close the ball around the cheese.

4 Roll the rice balls in the seasoned breadcrumbs until all are coated.

5 Preheat the air fryer to 400 degrees.

6 Place the rice balls in the air fryer basket and coat with cooking spray. Cook for 8 minutes, shake the basket, and cook another 7 minutes.

7 Heat the marinara sauce in a saucepan until warm. Serve sauce as a dip for arancini.

NOTE: If your rice balls are getting too dark without cooking through to the center, reduce the temperature to 380 degrees.

TIP: These are best made with day-old rice, which will hold together better than fresh-made rice.

VARY IT! Try any variety of cheese in the center or skip the cheese altogether.

VARY IT! Another great dip to serve with arancini is roasted red pepper sauce. Check out Chapter 18 for a quick and easy recipe.

Chapter **14**

Sweet Treats

Craving a sweet snack? You've come to the right place! From heart-healthy Honey-Roasted Mixed Nuts to decadent Fried Cannoli Wontons, this chapter has something for everyone!

We believe that air-fried foods have a powerful flavor component, especially some of the fruits that impart a large amount of natural sugar, so many of our recipes are made using a third of the amount of added sugar of their traditional counterparts. This doesn't mean we sacrifice the flavor or that sweetness you crave. Nope, not one bit!

Instead, we use our skills in the kitchen and knowledge of food to bring you a healthier alternative that's made with wholesome foods you can enjoy from the comfort of your own home. After all, a Pop Tart is still a Pop Tart, but when you air fry your own, it's made with much more love!

Honey-Roasted Mixed Nuts

PREP TIME: 5 MIN | COOK TIME: 15 MIN | YIELD: 8 SERVINGS

INGREDIENTS

½ cup raw, shelled pistachios

½ cup raw almonds

1 cup raw walnuts

2 tablespoons filtered water

2 tablespoons honey

1 tablespoon vegetable oil

2 tablespoons sugar

½ teaspoon salt

DIRECTIONS

1 Preheat the air fryer to 300 degrees.

2 Lightly spray an air-fryer-safe pan with olive oil; then place the pistachios, almonds, and walnuts inside the pan and place the pan inside the air fryer basket.

3 Cook for 15 minutes, shaking the basket every 5 minutes to rotate the nuts.

4 While the nuts are roasting, boil the water in a small pan and stir in the honey and oil. Continue to stir while cooking until the water begins to evaporate and a thick sauce is formed. *Note:* The sauce should stick to the back of a wooden spoon when mixed. Turn off the heat.

5 Remove the nuts from the air fryer (cooking should have just completed) and spoon the nuts into the stovetop pan. Use a spatula to coat the nuts with the honey syrup.

6 Line a baking sheet with parchment paper and spoon the nuts onto the sheet. Lightly sprinkle the sugar and salt over the nuts and let cool in the refrigerator for at least 2 hours.

7 When the honey and sugar have hardened, store the nuts in an airtight container in the refrigerator.

VARY IT! You can use whatever nuts you have on hand. If you prefer a maple-roasted nut, maple syrup instead of honey and omit the sugar.

Baked Apple Crisp

PREP TIME: 15 MIN	COOK TIME: 23 MIN	YIELD: 4 SERVINGS

INGREDIENTS

2 large Granny Smith apples, peeled, cored, and chopped

¼ cup granulated sugar

¼ cup plus 2 teaspoons flour, divided

2 teaspoons milk

¼ teaspoon cinnamon

¼ cup oats

¼ cup brown sugar

2 tablespoons unsalted butter

⅛ teaspoon baking powder

⅛ teaspoon salt

DIRECTIONS

1 Preheat the air fryer to 350 degrees.

2 In a medium bowl, mix the apples, the granulated sugar, 2 teaspoons of the flour, the milk, and the cinnamon.

3 Spray 4 oven-safe ramekins with cooking spray. Divide the filling among the four ramekins.

4 In a small bowl, mix the oats, the brown sugar, the remaining ¼ cup of flour, the butter, the baking powder, and the salt. Use your fingers or a pastry blender to crumble the butter into pea-size pieces. Divide the topping over the top of the apple filling. Cover the apple crisps with foil.

5 Place the covered apple crisps in the air fryer basket and cook for 20 minutes. Uncover and continue cooking for 3 minutes or until the surface is golden and crunchy.

NOTE: Granny Smith apples hold up best for baking, but feel free to use the apple of your choice.

VARY IT! If you love nuts, try adding chopped pecans or walnuts to the topping.

Apple Dumplings

| PREP TIME: 25 MIN | COOK TIME: 25 MIN | YIELD: 4 SERVINGS |

INGREDIENTS

1 Basic Pie Dough (see the following recipe)

4 medium Granny Smith or Pink Lady apples, peeled and cored

4 tablespoons sugar

4 teaspoons cinnamon

½ teaspoon ground nutmeg

4 tablespoons unsalted butter, melted

4 scoops ice cream, for serving

DIRECTIONS

1 Preheat the air fryer to 330 degrees.

2 Bring the pie crust recipe to room temperature.

3 Place the pie crust on a floured surface. Divide the dough into 4 equal pieces. Roll out each piece to ¼-inch-thick rounds. Place an apple onto each dough round. Sprinkle 1 tablespoon of sugar in the core part of each apple; sprinkle 1 teaspoon cinnamon and ⅛ teaspoon nutmeg over each. Place 1 table-spoon of butter into the center of each. Fold up the sides and fully cover the cored apples.

4 Place the dumplings into the air fryer basket and spray with cooking spray. Cook for 25 minutes. Check after 14 minutes cooking; if they're getting too brown, reduce the heat to 320 degrees and complete the cooking.

5 Serve hot apple dumplings with a scoop of ice cream.

NOTE: We grew up serving these with hot milk for a rustic and simple dessert.

Basic Pie Dough

PREP TIME: 10 MIN	COOK TIME: NONE	YIELD: 8 SERVINGS

INGREDIENTS

2½ cups all-purpose flour, plus extra for rolling

8 ounces cold unsalted butter

1 teaspoon salt

1 teaspoon sugar

½ teaspoon white vinegar

6 to 8 tablespoons ice water

DIRECTIONS

1. In a large bowl, place the flour. Grate the cold butter into the flour and add the salt and sugar. Using a pastry blender, cut the butter into the flour until you get small pea-size butter pieces.

2. Add in the vinegar. Working with 1 tablespoon of ice water at a time, add the water to the dough until the dough starts to hold together and you're able to form a ball with it.

3. Wrap the dough with plastic wrap and place in the refrigerator for at least 30 minutes and up to 1 day.

NOTE: If it's a hot day, place all the ingredients and equipment in the freezer for at least 30 minutes.

TIP: Make a double batch and store the extra batch in the freezer up to 3 months. This recipe is perfect for sweet and savory dishes!

Cherry Hand Pies

PREP TIME: 1 HR	COOK TIME: 8 MIN	YIELD: 8 SERVINGS

INGREDIENTS

4 cups frozen or canned pitted tart cherries (if using canned, drain and pat dry)

2 teaspoons lemon juice

½ cup sugar

¼ cup cornstarch

1 teaspoon vanilla extract

1 Basic Pie Dough (see the preceding recipe) or store-bought pie dough

DIRECTIONS

1 In a medium saucepan, place the cherries and lemon juice and cook over medium heat for 10 minutes, or until the cherries begin to break down.

2 In a small bowl, stir together the sugar and cornstarch. Pour the sugar mixture into the cherries, stirring constantly. Cook the cherry mixture over low heat for 2 to 3 minutes, or until thickened. Remove from the heat and stir in the vanilla extract. Allow the cherry mixture to cool to room temperature, about 30 minutes.

3 Meanwhile, bring the pie dough to room temperature. Divide the dough into 8 equal pieces. Roll out the dough to ¼-inch thickness in circles. Place ¼ cup filling in the center of each rolled dough. Fold the dough to create a half-circle. Using a fork, press around the edges to seal the hand pies. Pierce the top of the pie with a fork for steam release while cooking. Continue until 8 hand pies are formed.

4 Preheat the air fryer to 350 degrees.

5 Place a single layer of hand pies in the air fryer basket and spray with cooking spray. Cook for 8 to 10 minutes or until golden brown and cooked through.

TIP: Make a double batch and freeze the uncooked hand pies for a quick dessert any day of the week. Defrost hand pies and cook as above or cook frozen hand pies for 325 degrees for 20 minutes.

VARY IT! Change up the pie filling with any favorite pie filling. Our next favorite is rhubarb.

Wild Blueberry Sweet Empanadas

| PREP TIME: 4 HR 30 MIN | COOK TIME: 8 MIN | YIELD: 12 SERVINGS |

INGREDIENTS

2 cups frozen wild blueberries

5 tablespoons chia seeds

¼ cup honey

1 tablespoon lemon or lime juice

¼ cup water

1½ cups all-purpose flour

1 cup whole-wheat flour

½ teaspoon salt

1 tablespoon sugar

½ cup cold unsalted butter

1 egg

½ cup plus 2 tablespoons milk, divided

1 cup powdered sugar

1 teaspoon vanilla extract

DIRECTIONS

1 To make the wild blueberry chia jam, place the blueberries, chia seeds, honey, lemon or lime juice, and water into a blender and pulse for 2 minutes. Pour the chia jam into a glass jar or bowl and cover. Store in the refrigerator at least 4 to 8 hours or until the jam is thickened.

2 In a food processor, place the all-purpose flour, whole-wheat flour, salt, sugar, and butter and process for 2 minutes, scraping down the sides of the food processor every 30 seconds. Add in the egg and blend for 30 seconds. Using the pulse button, add in ½ cup of the milk 1 tablespoon at a time or until the dough is moist enough to handle and be rolled into a ball. Let the dough rest at room temperature for 30 minutes.

3 On a floured surface, cut the dough in half; then form a ball and cut each ball into 6 equal pieces, totaling 12 equal pieces. Work with one piece at a time, and cover the remaining dough with a towel. Roll out the dough into a 6-inch round, much like a tortilla, with ¼ inch thickness. Place 4 tablespoons of filling in the center of round, fold over to form a half-circle. Using a fork, crimp the edges together and pierce the top with a fork for air holes. Repeat with the remaining dough and filling.

4 Preheat the air fryer to 350 degrees.

5 Working in batches, place 3 to 4 empanadas in the air fryer basket and spray with cooking spray. Cook for 8 minutes. Repeat in batches, as needed. Allow the sweet empanadas to cool for 15 minutes. Meanwhile, in a small bowl, whisk together the powdered sugar, the remaining 2 tablespoons of milk, and the vanilla extract. Then drizzle the glaze over the surface and serve.

NOTE: These reheat well. If you want to freeze or store empanadas in the refrigerator, don't glaze them. Reheat them in the air fryer at 360 degrees for 12 minutes. You can also freeze without cooking, as well. Follow the same reheating instructions.

Vegan Brownie Bites

PREP TIME: 10 MIN	COOK TIME: 8 MIN	YIELD: 10 SERVINGS

INGREDIENTS

⅔ cup walnuts

⅓ cup all-purpose flour

¼ cup dark cocoa powder

⅓ cup cane sugar

¼ teaspoon salt

2 tablespoons vegetable oil

1 teaspoon pure vanilla extract

1 tablespoon almond milk

1 tablespoon powdered sugar

DIRECTIONS

1 Preheat the air fryer to 350 degrees.

2 To a blender or food processor fitted with a metal blade, add the walnuts, flour, cocoa powder, sugar, and salt. Pulse until smooth, about 30 seconds. Add in the oil, vanilla, and milk and pulse until a dough is formed.

3 Remove the dough and place in a bowl. Form into 10 equal-size bites.

4 Liberally spray the metal trivet in the air fryer basket with olive oil mist. Place the brownie bites into the basket and cook for 8 minutes, or until the outer edges begin to slightly crack.

5 Remove the basket from the air fryer and let cool. Sprinkle the brownie bites with powdered sugar and serve.

NOTE: Brownie bites will keep in an airtight container in the refrigerator for up to 10 days or in the freezer for up to 3 months.

White Chocolate Cranberry Blondies

PREP TIME: 10 MIN	COOK TIME: 18 MIN	YIELD: 6 SERVINGS

INGREDIENTS

⅓ cup butter

½ cup sugar

1 teaspoon vanilla extract

1 large egg

1 cup all-purpose flour

½ teaspoon baking powder

⅛ teaspoon salt

¼ cup dried cranberries

¼ cup white chocolate chips

DIRECTIONS

1 Preheat the air fryer to 320 degrees.

2 In a large bowl, cream the butter with the sugar and vanilla extract. Whisk in the egg and set aside.

3 In a separate bowl, mix the flour with the baking powder and salt. Then gently mix the dry ingredients into the wet. Fold in the cranberries and chocolate chips.

4 Liberally spray an oven-safe 7-inch springform pan with olive oil and pour the batter into the pan.

5 Cook for 17 minutes or until a toothpick inserted in the center comes out clean.

6 Remove and let cool 5 minutes before serving.

NOTE: Store in an airtight container on the counter for 5 days or in the refrigerator for 2 weeks.

TIP: For a healthier blondie with more fiber, use white whole-wheat flour instead of all-purpose flour.

VARY IT! Add raisins or your favorite dried berry.

Sea-Salted Caramel Cookie Cups

PREP TIME: 10 MIN	COOK TIME: 12 MIN	YIELD: 12 SERVINGS

INGREDIENTS

⅓ cup butter

¼ cup brown sugar

1 teaspoon vanilla extract

1 large egg

1 cup all-purpose flour

½ cup old-fashioned oats

½ teaspoon baking soda

¼ teaspoon salt

⅓ cup sea-salted caramel chips

DIRECTIONS

1 Preheat the air fryer to 300 degrees.

2 In a large bowl, cream the butter with the brown sugar and vanilla. Whisk in the egg and set aside.

3 In a separate bowl, mix the flour, oats, baking soda, and salt. Then gently mix the dry ingredients into the wet. Fold in the caramel chips.

4 Divide the batter into 12 silicon muffin liners. Place the cookie cups into the air fryer basket and cook for 12 minutes or until a toothpick inserted in the center comes out clean.

5 Remove and let cool 5 minutes before serving.

NOTE: Store in an airtight container on the counter for 5 days or in the refrigerator for 2 weeks.

TIP: For a healthier cookie with more fiber, use white whole-wheat flour instead of all-purpose flour.

VARY IT! Replace the caramel chips with chocolate chips or white chocolate chips.

Thumbprint Sugar Cookies

PREP TIME: 10 MIN	COOK TIME: 8 MIN	YIELD: 10 SERVINGS

INGREDIENTS

2½ tablespoons butter

⅓ cup cane sugar

1 teaspoon pure vanilla extract

1 large egg

1 cup all-purpose flour

½ teaspoon baking soda

¼ teaspoon salt

10 chocolate kisses

DIRECTIONS

1 Preheat the air fryer to 350 degrees.

2 In a large bowl, cream the butter with the sugar and vanilla. Whisk in the egg and set aside.

3 In a separate bowl, mix the flour, baking soda, and salt. Then gently mix the dry ingredients into the wet. Portion the dough into 10 balls; then press down on each with the bottom of a cup to create a flat cookie.

4 Liberally spray the metal trivet of an air fryer basket with olive oil mist.

5 Place the cookies in the air fryer basket on the trivet and cook for 8 minutes or until the tops begin to lightly brown.

6 Remove and immediately press the chocolate kisses into the tops of the cookies while still warm.

7 Let cool 5 minutes and then enjoy.

NOTE: Depending on the size of your air fryer, you may need to bake the cookies in multiple batches.

NOTE: Store in an airtight container on the counter for 5 days or in the refrigerator for 2 weeks.

TIP: For a healthier cookie with more fiber, use white whole-wheat flour instead of all-purpose flour.

Dark Chocolate Peanut Butter S'mores

PREP TIME: 2 MIN	COOK TIME: 6 MIN	YIELD: 4 SERVINGS

INGREDIENTS

4 graham cracker sheets

4 marshmallows

4 teaspoons chunky peanut butter

4 ounces dark chocolate

½ teaspoon ground cinnamon

DIRECTIONS

1 Preheat the air fryer to 390 degrees. Break the graham crackers in half so you have 8 pieces.

2 Place 4 pieces of graham cracker on the bottom of the air fryer. Top each with one of the marshmallows and bake for 6 or 7 minutes, or until the marshmallows have a golden brown center.

3 While cooking, slather each of the remaining graham crackers with 1 teaspoon peanut butter.

4 When baking completes, carefully remove each of the graham crackers, add 1 ounce of dark chocolate on top of the marshmallow, and lightly sprinkle with cinnamon. Top with the remaining peanut butter graham cracker to make the sandwich. Serve immediately.

VARY IT! Try using chocolate or cinnamon graham crackers for a unique twist! Or replace the peanut butter with Nutella.

Fried Cannoli Wontons

PREP TIME: 25 MIN	COOK TIME: 8 MIN	YIELD: 10 SERVINGS

INGREDIENTS

8 ounces Neufchâtel cream cheese

¼ cup powdered sugar

1 teaspoon vanilla extract

¼ teaspoon salt

¼ cup mini chocolate chips

2 tablespoons chopped pecans (optional)

20 wonton wrappers

¼ cup filtered water

DIRECTIONS

1 Preheat the air fryer to 370 degrees.

2 In a large bowl, use a hand mixer to combine the cream cheese with the powdered sugar, vanilla, and salt. Fold in the chocolate chips and pecans. Set aside.

3 Lay the wonton wrappers out on a flat, smooth surface and place a bowl with the filtered water next to them.

4 Use a teaspoon to evenly divide the cream cheese mixture among the 20 wonton wrappers, placing the batter in the center of the wontons.

5 Wet the tip of your index finger, and gently moisten the outer edges of the wrapper. Then fold each wrapper until it creates a secure pocket.

6 Liberally spray the air fryer basket with olive oil mist.

7 Place the wontons into the basket, and cook for 5 to 8 minutes. When the outer edges begin to brown, remove the wontons from the air fryer basket. Repeat cooking with remaining wontons.

8 Serve warm.

TIP: Depending on the style of air fryer you have, the wontons may take a shorter time to cook. You may need to adjust the temperature down to 350 degrees if you notice the wontons burning. Do a trial run on one if you want to double-check before baking them all.

TIP: Store in an airtight container in the refrigerator for up to 3 days for best consistency. Reheat in the air fryer at 350 degrees for 5 minutes.

Maple Cinnamon Cheesecake

PREP TIME: 10 MIN	COOK TIME: 12 MIN	YIELD: 4 SERVINGS

INGREDIENTS

6 sheets of cinnamon graham crackers

2 tablespoons butter

8 ounces Neufchâtel cream cheese

3 tablespoons pure maple syrup

1 large egg

½ teaspoon ground cinnamon

¼ teaspoon salt

DIRECTIONS

1 Preheat the air fryer to 350 degrees.

2 Place the graham crackers in a food processor and process until crushed into a flour. Mix with the butter and press into a mini air-fryer-safe pan lined at the bottom with parchment paper. Place in the air fryer and cook for 4 minutes.

3 In a large bowl, place the cream cheese and maple syrup. Use a hand mixer or stand mixer and beat together until smooth. Add in the egg, cinnamon, and salt and mix on medium speed until combined.

4 Remove the graham cracker crust from the air fryer and pour the batter into the pan.

5 Place the pan back in the air fryer, adjusting the temperature to 315 degrees. Cook for 18 minutes. Carefully remove when cooking completes. The top should be lightly browned and firm.

6 Keep the cheesecake in the pan and place in the refrigerator for 3 or more hours to firm up before serving.

NOTE: Be sure to put an oven mitt or towel down in the refrigerator so the pan doesn't melt your fridge!

NOTE: This cheesecake will stay fresh in an airtight container for up to 5 days in the refrigerator.

VARY IT! Prefer a different flavor? Swap in your favorite spices like pumpkin pie or apple pie for a seasonal twist.

Keto Cheesecake Cups

PREP TIME: 10 MIN | COOK TIME: 10 MIN | YIELD: 6 SERVINGS

INGREDIENTS

8 ounces cream cheese

¼ cup plain whole-milk Greek yogurt

1 large egg

1 teaspoon pure vanilla extract

3 tablespoons monk fruit sweetener

¼ teaspoon salt

½ cup walnuts, roughly chopped

DIRECTIONS

1 Preheat the air fryer to 315 degrees.

2 In a large bowl, use a hand mixer to beat the cream cheese together with the yogurt, egg, vanilla, sweetener, and salt. When combined, fold in the chopped walnuts.

3 Set 6 silicone muffin liners inside an air-fryer-safe pan. *Note: This is to allow for an easier time getting the cheesecake bites in and out. If you don't have a pan, you can place them directly in the air fryer basket.*

4 Evenly fill the cupcake liners with cheesecake batter.

5 Carefully place the pan into the air fryer basket and cook for about 10 minutes, or until the tops are lightly browned and firm.

6 Carefully remove the pan when done and place in the refrigerator for 3 hours to firm up before serving.

NOTE: Be sure to put an oven mitt or towel down in the refrigerator so the pan doesn't melt your fridge!

NOTE: You can use stevia in place of monk fruit sweetener to also comply with the keto diet compliance. If you aren't on a keto diet, you can use regular cane sugar in the place of the monk fruit.

TIP: Looking for a bit more fat on your keto diet? Add a tablespoon of MCT oil into the batter.

VARY IT! Have a favorite nut? Mix that into the batter, too!

3

The Part of Tens

Improve your total health with the air fryer.

Avoid common air fryer mistakes.

Use no-recipe recipes to create a perfect side for your main meal with the air fryer.

Make sauces to serve alongside your air fryer foods.

IN THIS CHAPTER

» Making healthy foods with the air fryer

» Surprising friends and family alike with how healthy the air fryer can be

Chapter **15**

Ten (or So) Ways to Improve Your Health with the Air Fryer

A large portion of how healthy you are is directly connected to the types of foods you're nourishing your body with.

Although the air fryer can certainly be used to swap some of the more calorically rich fare for healthier air-fried choices prepared at home, it can also be used in a multitude of other ways to improve your overall health.

In this chapter, we offer ten (or so) tips to ensure you're keeping your body in the best shape you can!

Soak Starchy Vegetables in Water

Soaking starchy foods — like potatoes, beets, and apples — in water for 30 minutes prior to air frying them can help decrease the levels of the compound acrylamide formed during cooking.

Research has linked higher intakes of acrylamide to certain cancers, and although there is room for more research, there's also a great opportunity to play it safe and soak your starchy foods. Soaking foods doesn't eliminate all the acrylamide, but it will significantly reduce it.

Use Salt Sparingly

Every individual has a different pallet and sensitivity to salt. Although salt is a necessary ingredient in recipes to help bring out the flavor of the food, it can also be used to excess. The standard American diet is too high in sodium, especially for those who eat a lot of fried foods and fast foods.

To help monitor the salt in the recipes in this book, we use just the right amount to deliver a very mild flavor. Tailor the recipes to your own pallet and, when needed, use additional salt sparingly.

Add One Vegetable to Every Meal

Vegetables pack a lot of bang for their nutritional buck. Increasing your intake of vegetables can provide an array of anti-inflammatory benefits that help prevent disease. Plus, vegetables are a great way to increase your fiber intake, too!

TIP

When preparing any of the Meaty Mains (Chapter 11) or Seafood Mains (Chapter 12), be sure to add in a vegetable or two! Check out Chapter 17 for quick no-recipe recipes to add to your plate.

Season with Herbs and Spices

Throughout the recipes in this book, we rarely rely on the help of canned or jarred sauces. Instead, we prefer to season foods with fresh or dried herbs and spices. Doing so keeps you in control of what ingredients are going in your foods. (Many shelf-stable sauces are high in added sugar and sodium and devoid of the flavor we long for you to achieve with the recipes.)

TIP

Chapter 2 offers some helpful tips on making your own seasoning blends.

Switch to Whole-Grain Breadcrumbs

We love crunchy, air-fried foods as much as the next person! But to increase the nutritional value a bit further, we love using whole-grain breadcrumbs. You can find them at most supermarkets, or make your own using whole-grain bread. The difference between whole-grain breadcrumbs and traditional breadcrumbs is extra fiber (as well as B vitamins).

Amp Up the Fiber

Another alternative, especially if you're following a gluten-free diet, is to use a flaxseed meal or nut-based coating for recipes with a breading. Both flaxseed and nuts, like walnuts, offer a wide variety of nutritional benefits, such as heart-healthy omega-3s and more fiber. They provide a slightly different flavor, though, so we suggest trying them out first with the Gluten-Free Nutty Chicken Fingers recipe in Chapter 11.

Experiment with Plant-Based Proteins

We aren't talking about the faux red-meat burgers here! Plant-based proteins range from lentils to soybeans to quinoa, and you can use the air fryer to create a delicious variety of meal choices that the entire family will love.

Not only is incorporating more plant-forward proteins good for your health (you'll be increasing your fiber intake as well as lowering your intake of saturated fat from animal proteins), but you'll also be helping the environment. A win-win for health on all accounts!

Eat Consistently

So often we hear clients say that they skip meals to stay healthy. We hate to break it to you, but this is not the best way to improve your health. Your body is like a car: It needs fuel to performs its daily activities. When you allow it to run on empty, it won't get you where you need to be.

Change your mind-set and nourish your body consistently with a well-balanced diet. Check out the hearty vegetable-forward sandwiches in Chapter 8 if you're tight on time.

Enjoy a Sweet Treat

Did you know that most diets that eliminate specific foods tend to fail? Plus, they cause dieters to gain back weight when they return to eating the foods they crave. Why go through the headache of all of that?

Instead, have your cake and eat it too — in moderation! The recipes in Chapter 14 show you how to create homemade desserts using your air fryer. We know how sweet Westernized desserts truly are, so we tested and retested multiple times to bring you the same sweet treat with lower added sugar. You're welcome!

Chapter **16**

Ten Mistakes to Avoid with Your Air Fryer

M aking the perfect air-fried food every time takes practice. If you've landed on this chapter, we really hope it's before you've charred your food to a crisp! When we were just starting out with our air fryers, we learned the hard way a few times.

But rest assured, we've learned from our mistakes and spent countless hours testing various models of the air fryer to compile these tips for you. Sit back, relax, and remember: With practice comes perfection!

Putting Food in an Unheated Basket

Don't worry: We write this tip as a step in every recipe so you don't have to guess for yourself when to turn the air fryer on (or wait an extra few minutes when your recipe is ready to go in).

Preheating the air fryer essentially allows the recipe to heat evenly when you put it in and be cooked to perfection by the time cooking completes. If you put food in an unheated basket, it may take longer to cook to the proper temperature, especially with foods like beef, chicken, and seafoods.

Overcrowding the Basket

Some recipes need to be cooked in batches. There's just no way around this (unless of course you decrease the recipe quantity and adjust ingredients accordingly). Be sure to allow space between the food (like chips, fries, and many of the starters in Chapter 7) so they achieve the perfect crisp every time.

Filling Your Cakes and Cupcakes Too High

When using a pan or air-fryer-safe dish inside the air fryer, make sure not to fill them too high. Fill the pan only three-quarters full. That way, you'll ensure that the pan doesn't overflow when cooking or hit the top of the air fryer unit when inserting it into the machine. Trust us, no one wants to scrape the top of a cheesecake off of an air fryer!

Undercooking Foods

Invest in a food thermometer so you can properly assure your raw foods have been cooked to the safe internal temperatures. Need a refresher? Check out Appendix B.

Multitasking without Watching the Time

We get it: You have a million things to do in addition to getting food on the table! But every second counts when you're air-frying foods. Set a timer in addition to the one on your air fryer (especially if you leave to go do the laundry in another room) so you don't forget about your recipe.

Preparing a Wet Batter for Breaded Foods

There's a reason we coat most of our breaded recipes in a panko, nut, or other dry crust. Moist batters don't work well with the air fryer. Because air-fried cooking uses significantly less oil than traditional deep-fried cooking, the batter needs to be dry when going into the air-fryer basket.

Forgetting to Shake the Basket

Shaking the basket prevents the food from overcooking on one side. It's easy to do but equally as easy to forget. We've found it helpful to use a timer on our smartphones to ensure we remember to shake, shake, shake!

Using the Wrong Kind of Cooking Oil

We often use extra-virgin olive oil, avocado oil, and sesame oil in our recipes because they have a high smoke point (meaning the oils can withstand high-heat cooking), making them perfect for air-fried cooking. Unrefined oils, such as flaxseed, wheat germ, and walnut oil have a low smoke point and shouldn't be heated.

Putting Off Cleaning Your Fryer

The best way to ensure you get the perfect air-fried foods is to make sure you're working with clean, well-functioning equipment. You can do this by cleaning your air fryer after each use. We promise, it's actually not as hard as it sounds. Most air fryers are very easy to clean and take 5 minutes, tops.

REMEMBER

Just be sure you've let the air-fryer basket cool completely before putting it in water, and don't put it in the dishwasher! Check out Chapter 1 for specifics on cleaning your air fryer.

Using Foods That Are Too Small

The air fryer you own is a set size. It's not something you can change (unless, of course, you buy a bigger one). Use the basket inside your air fryer to gauge what size to cut your vegetables and other smaller air-fried foods.

WARNING

You may see recipes elsewhere that tell you to cook popcorn in the air fryer, but we've tried it and disagree. The small kernels fall through most air-fryer baskets and make it challenging to cook evenly without burning.

Chapter **17**

Ten (or So) No-Recipe Recipes That Make Perfect Sides

I n this chapter, we share our magic formula for simple yet delectable sides. To create a spectacular accompaniment, all you really need is your favorite fruit or vegetable, plus some fresh herbs or spices, plus the right oil or vinaigrette (see Chapter 2). That's it!

After you try the ideas in this chapter, you'll be ready to create your own simple sides!

Brussels Sprouts with Bacon

If you've sworn off brussels sprouts, this side dish will tempt you back, we promise. The trick to get the bitterness out of brussels sprouts is to slice them in half and soak them in salted water for 5 minutes. Drain, pat dry, and spritz with extra-virgin olive oil. Then place them in the air fryer basket and top with chopped bacon pieces (about two strips chopped up). Cook for 10 to 12 minutes at 360 degrees. Then toss with a balsamic vinaigrette and serve hot.

Roasted Green Bean Salad

Green beans are an easy vegetable to find year-round. We love them, but we're the first to admit: They can get boring. This pairing is sure to shake things up! Just clean and cut green beans into 2-inch pieces. Toss with extra-virgin olive oil and put them in the air fryer for 6 to 8 minutes at 390 degrees. Then place the green beans in a serving bowl and add sliced cherry tomatoes, chopped red onion, and fresh parsley. Dress the salad with a squeeze or two of fresh lemon juice, extra-virgin olive oil, sea salt, cracked black pepper, and garlic powder. Served hot or cold, this dish is a family favorite.

Summer Succotash

When the summer sun is high and the farmers markets are packed with fresh produce, it's time to try this delicious side! Simply slice fresh zucchini, summer squash, sweet onions, and red bell peppers in bite-size pieces. Toss the veggies with extra-virgin olive oil, sea salt, and fresh thyme. Then cook in the air fryer for 20 minutes at 380 degrees. Serve hot out of the air fryer with a splash of red wine vinaigrette and grated Parmesan cheese.

Other favorite summertime veggies to add to this would be mushrooms, kohlrabi, leeks, fennel, and grape tomatoes.

Tomatoes with Fresh Burrata

Pick up a bag of seasonal tomatoes or grab a can of whole tomatoes. Either way, this preparation will wow your guests!

Roasting tomatoes give them a charred flavor and deepens their umami (meaty) flavor. Toss raw tomatoes with extra-virgin olive oil and sea salt. Then roast them in the air fryer or 25 minutes at 320 degrees, and another 5 minutes at 390 degrees. When they come out of the air fryer, toss them in a balsamic glaze. Serve the tomatoes over fresh burrata or fresh mozzarella cheese and top with chopped basil.

With the convenience of canned tomatoes, this dish can be served in winter, too! Canned, whole tomatoes need to be drained, and sliced lengthwise. Toss with extra-virgin olive oil and sea salt. Then place them on parchment paper before putting them into the air fryer. (Canned tomatoes have more liquid and you don't want the liquid to scorch on the bottom of the air fryer, so parchment paper helps!)

TECHNICAL STUFF

Research shows that tomatoes are loaded with lycopene, which is heart and prostate protective. Must be why tomatoes are at the heart of Mediterranean cuisine!

Savory Mushrooms

Umami-mia! Mushrooms hit our umami taste buds right in the heart! You can bread them, stuff them, or simply toss them before air frying and create a spectacular side or star appetizer. Talk about a versatile vegetable. Here are our favorite simple sides:

>> **Steakhouse:** Toss whole mushrooms with extra-virgin olive oil, Worcestershire sauce, and steak seasoning. Finish off with a drizzle of butter and chopped parsley.

>> **Asian Flare:** Toss whole mushrooms with sesame oil, soy sauce, and red pepper flakes. Finish off with a sprinkling of chopped green onions and sesame seeds.

>> **Italian:** Marinate mushrooms in balsamic vinegar for 10 minutes. Then drain and toss with extra-virgin olive oil. Finish with sea salt, fresh basil, and grated pecorino Romano cheese.

Whichever variety you choose, just pop them in the air fryer for 10 to 12 minutes at 380 degrees.

Crazy for Carrots

Carrots are perfect for the air fryer. You can make them into a chip (see Chapter 10), cut them into fries, or pair them with a variety of spices and herbs. Consider these fun combinations if you find yourself with an extra bag (or can) of carrots:

>> **Parmesan Roasted:** Slice the carrots, and toss them with extra-virgin olive oil, salt, and grated Parmesan cheese before placing in the air fryer.

>> **Slightly Sweet:** Slice the carrots, and toss them with extra-virgin olive oil, honey, and salt. Then place in the air fryer. Toss with chopped pecans and parsley before serving.

>> **Thyme:** Slice the carrots, and toss them with extra-virgin olive oil, salt, and dried thyme before placing in the air fryer.

Whichever variety you choose, put them in the air fryer for 15 to 20 minutes at 380 degrees.

Cheesy Zucchini

One of our favorite summertime veggies is crisp zucchini. Zucchini rounds spritzed with extra-virgin olive oil and topped with your favorite shredded cheese and maybe a sprinkling of herbs is a simple side. Our favorite combos are Parmesan and rosemary; gouda and chives; Monterey Jack and cumin; and mozzarella and basil. Cook for 12 minutes at 370 degrees.

If you don't happen to have a spiralizer you can pick up pre-spiralized zucchini. Toss them with extra-virgin olive oil and cook for 10 minutes at 330 degrees. Then toss with red wine vinegar, grated Parmesan cheese, and fresh parsley. Easy as 1-2-3!

Roasted Sweet Potatoes Three Ways

Roasted sweet potatoes can be served sweet, savory, and spicy. Cube a sweet potato, spritz with cooking oil, and then decide which option you prefer:

>> **Sweet:** Toss with brown sugar, cinnamon, salt, and coconut oil. Then place in the air fryer.

>> **Savory:** Toss with chopped rosemary, extra-virgin olive oil, cracked pepper, and salt. Then place in the air fryer.

>> **Spicy:** Mix with chopped jalapeño and a sprinkle of chipotle seasoning; then place in the air fryer. Then toss the cooked potatoes with chopped cilantro, lime, and avocado oil.

Whichever variety you prefer, cook in the air fryer for 10 to 12 minutes at 380 degrees.

Peaches and Pineapple and Pears! Oh, My!

You may not consider something sweet to be a suitable side dish, but the new school of thought is to serve your sweet with the meal. That's right, no need to wait until the end of the meal for something sweet.

Peaches, pineapple, and pears taste incredible when they get hit with a little heat. Check out these options:

>> **Just Peachy:** Pop a peach into the air fryer and cook for 5 minutes at 330 degrees. Top with cottage cheese and a drizzle of honey! This dish is great for breakfast, too!

>> **Tropical:** Grab a can of sliced pineapple and heat the rings for 5 minutes at 350 degrees. Serve with a sprinkling of toasted coconut flakes and chopped macadamia nuts.

>> **Fall Favorite:** Slice pears in spears and air fry 3 minutes at 360 degrees. Toss the heated pears with chopped pecans, crumbled goat cheese, and a drizzle of balsamic vinaigrette for a simple side salad.

Chapter 18

Ten Simple Sauces to Pair with Air-Fried Foods

Sauces can transform any plain meat or vegetable into something spectacular! Changing up the herbs or spices in a sauce is a simple way to elevate flavors and give the sauce a cultural twist. For instance, take a look at some popular herbs and spices that match a given cuisine:

» **Asian:** Ginger, peppers, sesame, soy sauce, sriracha, wasabi

» **French:** Chervil, chives, marjoram, nutmeg, tarragon, thyme

» **German:** Caraway, dill, juniper berry, mustard, paprika, parsley, thyme

» **Greek:** Basil, dill, mint, oregano, parsley, rosemary, saffron, sage, thyme

» **Indian:** Anise, cumin, curry, garam masala, ginger, saffron, turmeric

» **Italian:** Basil, bay leaf, lemon, oregano, parsley, sage

» **Mexican:** Coriander, cumin, hot sauce, lime, oregano, peppers

This list is just a starting point, but it's enough to give you some added leverage to ramp up the Creamy Brown Sauce into a mustardy brown sauce perfect for the German classic Pork Schnitzel (Chapter 11) or transform the Cool Cucumber Sauce into a Mexican Crema with the addition of lime, cumin, and hot sauce, perfect for the Beer-Breaded Halibut Fish Tacos (Chapter 12).

Creamy Brown Sauce

Heat 2 teaspoons extra-virgin olive oil in a deep skillet over medium heat. Add 1 tablespoon beef base (bouillon in a paste, not powdered), ½ cup water, and cracked pepper. Let this mixture simmer for 3 minutes, then remove from the heat and add 1 tablespoon unsalted butter and ¼ cup sour cream. Stir and serve.

Add 1 teaspoon prepared mustard for a German twist, or rosemary or thyme for an herb-infused addition.

Red Pepper Coulis

Canned red peppers or red peppers you roast yourself both can work in this sauce. To keep it simple, keep a jar of roasted red peppers on hand.

In a blender or food processor, place 1 cup roasted red bell peppers, ½ cup hot chicken stock or broth, 1 garlic clove, and ¼ teaspoon black pepper. Blend for 1 minute and drizzle in 2 tablespoons extra-virgin olive oil. Serve as a dip for breaded veggies, a pizza sauce, or over fresh pasta.

Add in fresh herbs, such as parsley, thyme, basil, or oregano, for a quick shift in flavor. Or add 2 tablespoons sour cream to make this sauce creamy.

Garlic Compound Butter

Compound butters are a great way to finish off cooked meat, like steak, shrimp, or fish, or elevate a sauce. Adding in a tablespoon of compound butter can give any warm sauce a glow. In a medium bowl, mix together ½ cup room-temperature unsalted butter, 1 tablespoon minced garlic, and ¼ teaspoon sea salt. Spoon the mixture on a piece of parchment paper and roll up into a log shape; refrigerate or freeze until ready to use.

Add your favorite fresh herb, lemon or lime zest, and cracked pepper.

Cucumber Yogurt Sauce

This cool and creamy sauce is a perfect, no-cook addition to cooked chicken, on top of a salad, or as a dip with your favorite vegetables. Combine 1 cup Greek yogurt with 1 grated cucumber, ½ teaspoon salt, 1 teaspoon dried dill, and 1 clove minced garlic.

Swap out the dill for cumin and add a splash of hot sauce and a squeeze of lime for a Mexican twist.

TIP

Pesto

Zesty pesto is great on pizza, with cooked shrimp, tossed with fresh pasta, or on cooked chicken. To keep your pesto perfectly bright green, blanch it: Add 2 cups basil to boiling water for 5 seconds and then quickly transfer it to ice water for 30 seconds. Pat the basil dry and add to a food processor. Top the basil with the juice from ½ lemon, and pulse for 10 seconds. Next, add in ½ cup grated Parmesan cheese, ⅓ cup pine nuts or walnuts, 1 clove garlic, and ½ teaspoon sea salt. Blend this mixture for 20 seconds then drizzle in ⅓ cup extra-virgin olive oil. Store in the refrigerator with a layer of oil on the surface.

Replace the basil with parsley, kale, spinach, or arugula if you like.

TIP

Chimichurri

Green chimichurri sauce is popular throughout Argentina and makes for a mouthwatering addition to grilled meats or vegetables. In a food processor, blend together 1½ cups fresh parsley, 2 tablespoons red wine vinegar, 2 cloves garlic, 1 teaspoon dried oregano, ½ teaspoon sea salt, ¼ teaspoon black pepper, and a pinch of red chili pepper flakes for 30 seconds. Then begin drizzling in ⅓ cup extra-virgin olive oil. Store in the refrigerator with a layer of oil over the top.

Cheesy Sauce

A basic cheese sauce begins with a *roux*, a mixture of butter and flour, melted together and lightly browned. Then you stir in milk and grated cheese. This sauce is incredibly versatile — use it as a sauce for vegetables, over roasted potatoes, or tossed with pasta.

In a heavy saucepan, heat 2 tablespoons all-purpose flour and 2 tablespoons unsalted butter over medium heat for 4 minutes, until the sauce turns a golden color. Whisk in 1 cup milk and cook for an additional 3 minutes until the sauce thickens; then add in 1½ cups grated cheddar, Monterey Jack, or mozzarella cheese. Stir until a thick sauce forms. Serve immediately.

Simple Ranch Dressing

Ranch dressing is an American favorite. It's also an easy dressing or sauce to make on your own! In a blender or food processor, blend together the following ingredients until smooth and creamy: ½ cup mayonnaise, 1 cup Greek yogurt, ¼ cup milk, 1 teaspoon dried dill, 1 tablespoon parsley, ¼ teaspoon onion powder, ½ teaspoon garlic powder, and salt and pepper to taste. Store in the refrigerator up to 5 days.

TIP

Add in hot sauce, chopped jalapeño peppers, or taco seasoning to kick it up a notch.

Classic Vinaigrette

Learning how to make a simple vinaigrette can save you time and money. Plus, vinaigrette is a great topping for air-fried foods!

In a small bowl, add 3 tablespoons extra-virgin olive oil and 2 tablespoons vinegar (red, white wine, or cider). Add in 1 teaspoon prepared mustard, 1 minced shallot, and 1 tablespoon chopped parsley. Whisk and serve.

TIP

Mix things up by changing the vinegar and adding in different herbs, like basil, oregano, or tarragon.

Creamy Avocado Dressing

Smooth and delicious avocados are jam-packed full of vitamins, minerals, healthy fats, and flavor. This dressing makes for a great pasta sauce, salad dressing, veggie dip, or sauce on your favorite air-fried meats.

Using a blender or food processor, blend together the following ingredients until smooth and creamy: ½ avocado, ¼ cup sour cream or Greek yogurt, ¼ cup water, 2 tablespoons lemon juice, ½ teaspoon ground cumin, and salt to taste.

TIP

Blend in 1 cup fresh chopped parsley, cilantro, or basil for a different flavor.

4

Appendixes

Appendix A

Metric Conversion Guide

Note: The recipes in this book weren't developed or tested using metric measurements. There may be some variation in quality when converting to metric units.

Common Abbreviations

Abbreviation(s)	What It Stands For
cm	Centimeter
C., c.	Cup
G, g	Gram
kg	Kilogram
L, l	Liter
lb.	Pound
mL, ml	Milliliter
oz.	Ounce
pt.	Pint
t., tsp.	Teaspoon
T., Tb., Tbsp.	Tablespoon

Volume

U.S. Units	Canadian Metric	Australian Metric
¼ teaspoon	1 milliliter	1 milliliter
½ teaspoon	2 milliliters	2 milliliters
1 teaspoon	5 milliliters	5 milliliters
1 tablespoon	15 milliliters	20 milliliters
¼ cup	50 milliliters	60 milliliters
⅓ cup	75 milliliters	80 milliliters
½ cup	125 milliliters	125 milliliters
⅔ cup	150 milliliters	170 milliliters
¾ cup	175 milliliters	190 milliliters
1 cup	250 milliliters	250 milliliters
1 quart	1 liter	1 liter
1½ quarts	1.5 liters	1.5 liters
2 quarts	2 liters	2 liters
2½ quarts	2.5 liters	2.5 liters
3 quarts	3 liters	3 liters
4 quarts (1 gallon)	4 liters	4 liters

Weight

U.S. Units	Canadian Metric	Australian Metric
1 ounce	30 grams	30 grams
2 ounces	55 grams	60 grams
3 ounces	85 grams	90 grams
4 ounces (¼ pound)	115 grams	125 grams
8 ounces (½ pound)	225 grams	225 grams
16 ounces (1 pound)	455 grams	500 grams (½ kilogram)

Length

Inches	Centimeters
0.5	1.5
1	2.5
2	5.0
3	7.5
4	10.0
5	12.5
6	15.0
7	17.5
8	20.5
9	23.0
10	25.5
11	28.0
12	30.5

Temperature (Degrees)

Fahrenheit	Celsius
32	0
212	100
250	120
275	140
300	150
325	160
350	180
375	190
400	200
425	220
450	230
475	240
500	260

Appendix B

Safe Cooking Temperatures

For food safety, it's always wise to have a thermometer on hand to test the inner temperature of the foods you're preparing. Use this as a guide to ensure your recipes come to the proper temperature, especially for the meats in Chapter 11, to prevent foodborne illness. You can apply these cooking temperatures to the recipes you make outside the air fryer as well.

Cooking Temperatures

Food	Temperature (°F)
Eggs	145
Red meat (whole)	145
Red meat (ground)	160
Pork	145
Poultry	165
Seafood	145
Casseroles or leftovers	165

Index

About the Authors

Wendy Jo Peterson, MS, RDN: Wendy Jo is an award-winning author, speaker, culinary nutritionist, proud military wife, and mom. Whether at work or at the table, Wendy Jo believes in savoring life. Check out her most popular books: *Born to Eat: Whole, Healthy Foods from Baby's First Bite*, written with Leslie Schilling (Skyhorse), and *Mediterranean Diet Cookbook For Dummies*, written with Meri Raffetto (Wiley). When she's not in her kitchen, you can find Wendy Jo strolling the beach with her Labradors and daughter or exploring the great outdoors in #OlafTheCampervan. You can catch her on social media at @just_wendyjo or check out her website, www.justwendyjo.com.

Elizabeth Shaw, MS, RDN, CLT, CPT: Liz is a national nutrition expert, bestselling author, and media dietitian who works as a spokesperson and nutrition professor. Her passion for breaking down science-based facts into digestible sound bites has led her to what she loves doing most: helping others understand the important role nutrition can play in their lifelong health. Her first work, *Fertility Foods Cookbook: 100+ Recipes to Nourish Your Body*, written with Sara Haas (Hatherleigh Press), is a must-have for those on the journey to baby. You can find Liz sharing her recipes on her website, www.shawsimpleswaps.com, or over on social media at @shawsimpleswaps with her #ShawKitchen crew (Mr. CEO, her husband, and H, her daughter!).

Dedication

To our daughters and husbands, Miss A, H, Brandon, and Wayne, thank you for supporting our love for food and sharing that with the world! To our family and friends, the best taste testers around. And to every person who longs to create that crispy, crunchy restaurant-style food from the comfort of your own home, pajamas permitted. We hope you enjoy this book as much as we loved creating it for you!

Authors' Acknowledgments

We would like to acknowledge our agent, Matt Wagner, for bringing this incredible project to us. We're forever grateful for Tracy Boggier, Senior Acquisitions Editor at Wiley, who believed in us and the power of two registered dietitian nutritionists to create an entire collection of recipes using the air fryer. We appreciate the support we've received throughout this project. It's forever cherished.

Publisher's Acknowledgments

Senior Acquisitions Editor: Tracy Boggier

Project Editor: Elizabeth Kuball

Copy Editor: Elizabeth Kuball

Proofreader: Debbye Butler

Production Editor: Mohammed Zafar Ali

Cover Image: Courtesy of Wendy Jo Peterson and Elizabeth Shaw

Take dummies with you everywhere you go!

Whether you are excited about e-books, want more from the web, must have your mobile apps, or are swept up in social media, dummies makes everything easier.

Find us online!

Leverage the power

Dummies is the global leader in the reference category and one of the most trusted and highly regarded brands in the world. No longer just focused on books, customers now have access to the dummies content they need in the format they want. Together we'll craft a solution that engages your customers, stands out from the competition, and helps you meet your goals.

Advertising & Sponsorships

Connect with an engaged audience on a powerful multimedia site, and position your message alongside expert how-to content. Dummies.com is a one-stop shop for free, online information and know-how curated by a team of experts.

- Targeted ads
- Video
- Email Marketing
- Microsites
- Sweepstakes sponsorship

20 MILLION PAGE VIEWS EVERY SINGLE MONTH

15 MILLION UNIQUE VISITORS PER MONTH

43% OF ALL VISITORS ACCESS THE SITE VIA THEIR MOBILE DEVICES

700,000 NEWSLETTER SUBSCRIPTION TO THE INBOXES OF
300,000 UNIQUE INDIVIDUALS EVERY WEEK

# of dummies

Custom Publishing

Reach a global audience in any language by creating a solution that will differentiate you from competitors, amplify your message, and encourage customers to make a buying decision.

- Apps
- Books
- eBooks
- Video
- Audio
- Webinars

Brand Licensing & Content

Leverage the strength of the world's most popular reference brand to reach new audiences and channels of distribution.

For more information, visit dummies.com/biz

PERSONAL ENRICHMENT

Staying Sharp
9781119187790
USA $26.00
CAN $31.99
UK £19.99

Facebook
9781119179030
USA $21.99
CAN $25.99
UK £16.99

Guitar
9781119293354
USA $24.99
CAN $29.99
UK £17.99

Investing
9781119293347
USA $22.99
CAN $27.99
UK £16.99

Beekeeping
9781119310068
USA $22.99
CAN $27.99
UK £16.99

Digital Photography
9781119235606
USA $24.99
CAN $29.99
UK £17.99

Meditation
9781119251163
USA $24.99
CAN $29.99
UK £17.99

Pregnancy
9781119235491
USA $26.99
CAN $31.99
UK £19.99

Samsung Galaxy S7
9781119279952
USA $24.99
CAN $29.99
UK £17.99

iPhone
9781119283133
USA $24.99
CAN $29.99
UK £17.99

Crocheting
9781119287117
USA $24.99
CAN $29.99
UK £16.99

Nutrition
9781119130246
USA $22.99
CAN $27.99
UK £16.99

PROFESSIONAL DEVELOPMENT

Windows 10
9781119311041
USA $24.99
CAN $29.99
UK £17.99

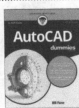

AutoCAD
9781119255796
USA $39.99
CAN $47.99
UK £27.99

Excel 2016
9781119293439
USA $26.99
CAN $31.99
UK £19.99

QuickBooks 2017
9781119281467
USA $26.99
CAN $31.99
UK £19.99

macOS Sierra
9781119280651
USA $29.99
CAN $35.99
UK £21.99

LinkedIn
9781119251132
USA $24.99
CAN $29.99
UK £17.99

Windows 10
9781119310563
USA $34.00
CAN $41.99
UK £24.99

SharePoint 2016
9781119181705
USA $29.99
CAN $35.99
UK £21.99

Fundamental Analysis
9781119263593
USA $26.99
CAN $31.99
UK £19.99

Networking
9781119257769
USA $29.99
CAN $35.99
UK £21.99

Office 2016
9781119293477
USA $26.99
CAN $31.99
UK £19.99

Office 365
9781119265313
USA $24.99
CAN $29.99
UK £17.99

Salesforce.com
9781119239314
USA $29.99
CAN $35.99
UK £21.99

Coding
9781119293323
USA $29.99
CAN $35.99
UK £21.99